JN492302

Developing Listening Skills

2

Developing Listening Skills Book 2

Publisher	Chung Kyudo
Editors	Kim Jinsuk, Cho Sangik
Author	Michael A. Putlack
Designers	Yoon Jiyoung, Park Sunyoung

First published in January 2014
By Darakwon, Inc.
Darakwon Bldg., 211, Munbal-ro, Paju-si, Gyeonggi-do 10881
Republic of Korea
Tel: 82-2-736-2031 (Ext. 250)
Fax: 82-2-732-2037

ISBN 978-89-277-0705-9 58740
978-89-277-0701-1 58740 (set)

www.darakwon.co.kr

Components Main Book / Workbook
15 14 13 12 11 10 9 26 27 28 29 30

Developing Listening Skills

Workbook

2

DARAKWON

Chapter 1

Amazing Places

Unit 01 The Amazon Rainforest

A Listen to the talk on page 12 again. Then, write the answers to the questions.

1 Where does the Amazon River start?

____

2 About how many plant species live in the Amazon Rainforest?

____

3 How many types of insects are found in the Amazon Rainforest?

____

4 What humans live in the Amazon Rainforest?

____

5 How do the people living in the Amazon Rainforest get food?

____

B Use the words in the box to complete the sentences.

vegetation	surround	make contact with	gather	wildlife

1 We will try to ________________ the survivors of the crash tonight.

2 Everyone will ________________ by the fire and tell stories.

3 There is a lot of ________________ growing in the forest.

4 What kind of ________________ lives in this area?

5 The soldiers will ________________ the army and get ready to attack it from all sides.

C Listen to the talk on page 14 again. Then, circle the correct answers.

1 Victoria Falls is located in (North America / Africa).

2 Angel Falls is found deep in the (jungle / desert) in Venezuela.

3 Angel Falls is the world's (highest / widest) waterfall.

4 Many tourists (drive / hike) on the ground to get to Victoria Falls.

5 The teacher thinks that Victoria Falls is a (breathtaking / disappointing) sight.

D Listen to the talk. Then, write F (fact) or O (opinion) in each blank.

Notes

1 ______ Temperatures in the Sahara Desert are often more than forty degrees Celsius.

2 ______ The tourists are going to take a trip in the desert today.

3 ______ The tourists are going to have an amazing time.

Unit 02 The Grand Canyon

A **Listen to the talk on page 16 again. Then, write the answers to the questions.**

1 How did the Colorado River form the Grand Canyon?

____

2 Where is the Grand Canyon?

____

3 How deep is the Grand Canyon in some places?

____

4 Who lives in the Grand Canyon today?

____

5 How many people visit the Grand Canyon each year?

____

B **Use the words in the box to complete the sentences.**

majority	erode	tribe	protected area	rim

1 A ________________ of the people voted for Kelly for mayor.

2 That Native American belongs to the Cherokee ________________.

3 The land will ________________ if the river keeps flowing through it.

4 Look out at the Grand Canyon from the northern ________________.

5 This is a ________________, so hunting and fishing are not allowed.

C Listen to the talk on page 18 again. Then, choose the correct answers.

1 The listeners are going to go rafting down the ________________.

ⓐ Colorado River ⓑ Gulf of California ⓒ Grand Canyon

2 They will see the Grand Canyon from the ________________.

ⓐ top ⓑ side ⓒ bottom

3 They are going to go rafting in ________________ water.

ⓐ calm ⓑ fast ⓒ muddy

4 They will stop to look at some ________________.

ⓐ rocks ⓑ ruins ⓒ reflections

5 They are going to ________________ at the bottom of the Grand Canyon.

ⓐ camp ⓑ have lunch ⓒ swim

D Listen to the talk. Then, write F (fact) or O (opinion) in each blank.

Notes

1 ______ Yellowstone National Park is in three American states.

2 ______ People should go to Yellowstone National Park if they can.

3 ______ Visitors can see wildlife such as bears, elk, and wolves.

Unit 03
The Serengeti

A Listen to the talk on page 20 again. Then, write the answers to the questions.

1 In which part of Africa is the Serengeti?

____

2 What does most of the Serengeti look like?

____

3 What are some of the large animals that live in the Serengeti?

____

4 How large are some herds of zebras and gazelles?

____

5 Which great cats live in the Serengeti?

____

B Use the words in the box to complete the sentences.

wooded area	vast	prowl	is teeming with	herd

1 There is a ____________ jungle in this part of Africa.

2 The farmer has a large ____________ of cows on his farm.

3 Some people are cutting down trees in the ____________.

4 Many animals ____________ in this region at night.

5 The forest ____________ all sorts of animals.

C Listen to the talk on page 22 again. Then, fill in the blanks with the correct words.

1 The Great ________________ takes place in the Serengeti every year.

2 The animals migrate because of the rain ________________ in the area.

3 More than one ________________ wildebeests make the trip.

4 Lots of ________________ such as lions follow the animals making the trip.

5 There are also rivers full of ________________.

D Listen to the talk. Then, read a part of the talk and choose the correct paraphrase.

Notes

Large numbers of mammals and birds make their homes in this region, too. Unfortunately, since so much farming goes on there, some of the native animals are in danger of going extinct.

ⓐ There are lots of animals that live in the Pampas.
ⓑ Because of farmers, many mammals and birds from the Pampas are now extinct.
ⓒ Some of the mammals and birds in the Pampas may go extinct.

Unit 04

The Dead Sea

A **Listen to the talk on page 24 again. Then, write the answers to the questions.**

1 Where is the Dead Sea?

____

2 About how long is the Dead Sea?

____

3 What lives in the Dead Sea?

____

4 What happens to fish that swim into the Dead Sea?

____

5 How can people easily float on the water of the Dead Sea?

____

B **Use the words in the box to complete the sentences.**

border	salt content	sea level	evaporate	notable

1 There are many soldiers on the ____________ between those two countries.

2 That mountain is more than 3,000 meters above ____________.

3 The water will ____________ when the sun is shining.

4 Do you know the ____________ of the ocean?

5 One ____________ person in the city is Dr. Thompson.

C Listen to the talk on page 26 again. Then, answer T (true) or F (false).

1 ______ They are going to sail around some reefs near Belize.

2 ______ The Great Blue Hole is about 300 meters in diameter.

3 ______ The Great Blue Hole goes down 12 kilometers.

4 ______ The Great Blue Hole is too dangerous for scuba diving.

5 ______ The listeners will do some snorkeling at a reef.

D Listen to the talk. Then, read a part of the talk and choose the correct paraphrase.

Notes

> Orda Cave has passages that are a little more than five kilometers long. And virtually the entire cave is underwater.

ⓐ All of Orda Cave, which is five kilometers long, is underwater.
ⓑ Most of Orda Cave's five kilometers of passages are underwater.
ⓒ Orda Cave has passages that stretch for around five kilometers.

Chapter 2

Great Scientists

Unit 05

Hippocrates

A **Listen to the talk on page 30 again. Then, write the answers to the questions.**

1 How long did most people live thousands of years ago?

____

2 Where was Hippocrates from?

____

3 What do people call Hippocrates?

____

4 What did Hippocrates think about sicknesses and diseases?

____

5 When do people take the Hippocratic Oath?

____

B **Use the words in the box to complete the sentences.**

deity	passed away	superstition	based on	transform

1 One ______________ from Greek times was Zeus.

2 A common American ______________ is that breaking a mirror is bad luck.

3 This machine can ______________ raw materials into finished products.

4 Janet's grandmother ______________ last weekend.

5 This is a work of fiction, but it is ______________ a true story.

C Listen to the talk on page 32 again. Then, circle the correct answers.

1 Galen was the greatest (warrior / physician) in the Roman Empire.

2 Galen studied (medicine / law) in Alexandria.

3 Galen became a surgeon for (gladiators / soldiers) in the arena.

4 Galen was the personal doctor for Emperor (Nero / Marcus Aurelius).

5 Galen focused on (anatomy / biology) in his studies.

D Listen to the talk. Then, write T (true) or F (false) for the following statements about polio.

Notes

1 ______ Dr. Jonas Salk had polio when he was a child.

2 ______ Dr. Jonas Salk created a vaccine for polio.

3 ______ Today, polio is no longer a major problem.

Unit 06 Nicholas Copernicus

A Listen to the talk on page 34 again. Then, write the answers to the questions.

1 What did Aristotle think about Earth?

____

2 When did Nicholas Copernicus live?

____

3 What problem did Nicholas Copernicus have with Aristotle's model of the universe?

____

4 What was at the center of the solar system in Nicholas Copernicus's model?

____

5 What was the title of Nicholas Copernicus's book?

____

B Use the words in the box to complete the sentences.

geocentric	calculation	are fascinated by	astronomy	heliocentric

1 The children ______________ the pandas at the zoo.

2 In the ______________ model, all of the planets and stars move around Earth.

3 Joe's hobby is ______________, so he owns a couple of telescopes.

4 You made a mistake, so please do the ______________ one more time.

5 The ______________ model is the correct model of the solar system.

C Listen to the talk on page 36 again. Then, choose the correct answers.

1 The listeners are at ________________.

ⓐ an observatory ⓑ a college ⓒ a park

2 Johannes Kepler figured out how ________________ orbits the sun.

ⓐ Venus ⓑ Mars ⓒ Earth

3 Johannes Kepler was a ________________ astronomer.

ⓐ French ⓑ German ⓒ Polish

4 Johannes Kepler realized that the orbit of Mars was ________________.

ⓐ an ellipse ⓑ a circle ⓒ a square

5 Johannes Kepler discovered the three laws of planetary ________________.

ⓐ motion ⓑ appearance ⓒ gravity

D Listen to the talk. Then, write T (true) or F (false) for the following statements about William Herschel.

Notes

1 ______ He lived in both Germany and England.

2 ______ He made and sold many telescopes.

3 ______ He discovered the planet Neptune.

Unit 07

Albert Einstein

A Listen to the talk on page 38 again. Then, write the answers to the questions.

1 What kind of a student was Albert Einstein?

____

2 What was Albert Einstein doing when he published some papers in 1905?

____

3 What does $E = mc^2$ describe?

____

4 When did Albert Einstein receive the Nobel Prize in Physics?

____

5 Why did Albert Einstein leave Germany?

____

B Use the words in the box to complete the sentences.

drop out of	average	free time	matter	theory

1 The ________________ person today lives for more than seventy years.

2 Please tell us your ________________ about what happened last night.

3 It is impossible for ________________ to be created or destroyed.

4 In Sue's ________________, she often reads books or writes in her diary.

5 Do not ________________ school, or you will have trouble finding a job.

C Listen to the talk on page 40 again. Then, fill in the blanks with the correct words.

1 ________________ began to build up its military in the 1930s.

2 In 1939, ________________ began with the invasion of Poland.

3 Albert Einstein did not want Germany to make its own ________________.

4 The ________________ was the name of the American atomic bomb project.

5 In 1945, the Atomic Age began when the Americans ________________ an atomic bomb.

D Listen to the talk. Then, put the sentences in the correct order.

Notes

1 ______ Robert Oppenheimer received a PhD in Physics.

2 ______ Robert Oppenheimer said, “Now, I am become Death, the destroyer of worlds.”

3 ______ Robert Oppenheimer became the director of the lab in Los Alamos.

Unit 08 Marie Curie

A **Listen to the talk on page 42 again. Then, write the answers to the questions.**

1 Where was Marie Curie from?

____

2 Who was Marie Curie's husband?

____

3 What happened to Marie Curie's husband?

____

4 Why did Marie Curie receive the Nobel Prize in Chemistry?

____

5 What did Marie Curie help invent?

____

B **Use the words in the box to complete the sentences.**

element	radiation	is awarded	native	portable

1 The prize ____________ to the student with the best entry in the contest.

2 The most common ____________ in the atmosphere is nitrogen.

3 A laptop is a ____________ computer.

4 ____________ is dangerous, but it has a number of important uses.

5 Paul is a ____________ of England, but he lives in Italy today.

C Listen to the talk on page 44 again. Then, answer T (true) or F (false).

1 ______ Marie Curie died in 1834.

2 ______ Marie Curie won a Nobel Prize in physics and chemistry.

3 ______ Marie Curie probably died because of radiation.

4 ______ There were many studies on radiation in the early 1900s.

5 ______ Radiation can be dangerous to people.

D Listen to the talk. Then, put the sentences in the correct order.

Notes

1 ______ Pierre and Marie Curie got married.

2 ______ Pierre Curie did some work on quartz crystals and magnetism.

3 ______ A carriage ran over Pierre Curie and killed him.

Chapter 3

Historical Eras

Unit 09 The Stone Age

A Listen to the talk on page 48 again. Then, write the answers to the questions.

1 What is the longest period of time in human history called?

____

2 Where did humanoids live three million years ago?

____

3 What are the three periods in the Stone Age?

____

4 When did the second period in the Stone Age end?

____

5 When did humans learn to tame animals and start farming?

____

B Use the words in the box to complete the sentences.

tame	hunter-gatherers	fairly	permanent settlement	primitive

1 ______________ did not know how to farm the land at all.

2 The first ______________ was probably somewhere in the Middle East.

3 The tribesmen did not have any technology, so they lived ______________ lives.

4 Dogs and cats are ______________ animals and often live with humans.

5 I am ______________ certain that I answered all of the questions.

C Listen to the talk on page 50 again. Then, circle the correct answers.

1 The (Bronze / Gold) Age began after the Neolithic Period ended.

2 An alloy is a combination of two or more (stones / metals).

3 The Bronze Age started in (Egypt / China) around 3300 B.C.

4 People developed (writing / communication) systems during the Bronze Age.

5 After the Bronze Age ended, the (Steel / Iron) Age began.

D Listen to the talk. Then, answer the question.

Notes

Why does the speaker mention Egypt and Mesopotamia?

ⓐ To say that the Iron Age began in those places

ⓑ To compare those cultures with India and China

ⓒ To say that people there made many bronze objects

Unit 10 Ancient Greece

A **Listen to the talk on page 52 again. Then, write the answers to the questions.**

1 What did the ancient Greeks found?

____

2 What did Homer compose?

____

3 What was the greatest Greek city-state?

____

4 What were three other Greek city-states?

____

5 What did Alexander the Great do?

____

B **Use the words in the box to complete the sentences.**

epic poem	establish	warrior	statesman	the known world

1 We want to ______________ a new city by the ocean.

2 That man served his country well and became a great ______________.

3 In Greek mythology, Ajax was a ______________ who won many battles.

4 This ______________ tells about the Trojan War.

5 His goal was to visit many places in ______________.

C **Listen to the talk on page 54 again. Then, choose the correct answers.**

1 In 480 B.C., King Xerxes of ________________ invaded Greece.

ⓐ Persia ⓑ India ⓒ Egypt

2 King Xerxes's army had to go through ________________ to get into Greece.

ⓐ Thermopylae ⓑ Marathon ⓒ Actium

3 A force of ________________ Spartans blocked the enemy army.

ⓐ 300 ⓑ 3,000 ⓒ 30,000

4 Leonidas said, "________________," when King Xerxes told the Spartans to drop their weapons.

ⓐ *Eureka* ⓑ *Molon labe* ⓒ *Arma virumque cano*

5 How long did the Spartans hold out against the enemy?

ⓐ For 1 day ⓑ For 2 days ⓒ For 3 days

D **Listen to the talk. Then, answer the question.**

Notes

Why does the speaker discuss Sparta?

ⓐ To talk about its military victories

ⓑ To describe Spartan society

ⓒ To say where in Greece it was located

Unit 11

The Middle Ages

A Listen to the talk on page 56 again. Then, write the answers to the questions.

1 When did the Middle Ages last?

____

2 What happened to knowledge from Rome in the Middle Ages?

____

3 Who did Christian Europeans have to defend themselves against?

____

4 What did Charles Martel do?

____

5 What was a common system of government in the Middle Ages?

____

B Use the words in the box to complete the sentences.

conquer	dominate	barbarian	steadily	revolves around

1 The army hopes to ______________ the enemy by the end of the week.

2 Many ______________ tribes used to exist in Europe.

3 Society in that country ______________ a small government.

4 The child is ______________ getting better from his illness.

5 John expects to ______________ everyone else at the sporting event.

C **Listen to the talk on page 58 again. Then, fill in the blanks with the correct words.**

1 People in China started getting ________________ spots on their bodies in 1328.

2 The bubonic plague was a very ________________ disease.

3 The bubonic plague arrived in Europe and started the ________________.

4 Around thirty to ________________ percent of all Europeans died.

5 There were a few ________________ results after the Black Death ended.

D **Listen to the talk. Then, choose the correct connecting words for the sentences.**

Notes

1 Pope Urban II made a speech (and / but) called on people to travel to Jerusalem.

2 (After that / Because), many Europeans joined armies.

3 Some crusades were successful, (so / but) others were terrible failures.

Unit 12 The Renaissance

A **Listen to the talk on page 60 again. Then, write the answers to the questions.**

1 What did many Byzantines do in the 1300s?

____

2 When did the Renaissance start?

____

3 Where did the Renaissance begin?

____

4 What was a primary feature of the Renaissance?

____

5 What was a Renaissance Man?

____

B **Use the words in the box to complete the sentences.**

flee	is in decline	brilliant	relearn	excel

1 The country ________________ because of its corrupt politicians.

2 You must ________________ these math problems before you can solve more difficult ones.

3 Those students ________________ at computer programming.

4 Most animals ________________ when they see a dangerous animal near them.

5 Fred is a ________________ man, so he has many great ideas.

C Listen to the talk on page 62 again. Then, answer T (true) or F (false).

1 ______ The exhibit has art from the Middle Ages.

2 ______ Medieval art often used mythology as a topic.

3 ______ Renaissance artists often used perspective.

4 ______ The exhibit has works by Michelangelo and Botticelli.

5 ______ The director will teach the listeners how to paint.

D Listen to the talk. Then, choose the correct connecting words for the sentences.

Notes

1 The Renaissance started in Italy (or / and) was popular in many city-states there.

2 The Renaissance moved north, (but / so) it influenced France, Germany, and England.

3 The printing press let people print books quickly, (so / because) this let knowledge travel fast.

Chapter 4

Landmarks

Unit 13

The Eiffel Tower

A Listen to the talk on page 66 again. Then, write the answers to the questions.

1 Why did the organizers of the World's Fair build the Eiffel Tower?

____

2 How high is the Eiffel Tower?

____

3 What did the people of Paris think about the Eiffel Tower in the 1800s?

____

4 How did the French use the Eiffel Tower?

____

5 How do the people of Paris feel about the Eiffel Tower today?

____

B Use the words in the box to complete the sentences.

eyesore	impress	imposing	manmade structure	tons

1 Some dinosaurs used to weigh many ______________.

2 That pile of garbage is an ______________, so please get rid of it.

3 Kevin is so large that he is an ______________ figure.

4 You will ______________ me if you finish the work by tonight.

5 The archaeologists found a ______________ in the middle of the jungle.

C Listen to the talk on page 68 again. Then, circle the correct answers.

1 George Washington led the Americans to victory in the (Revolutionary / Civil) War.

2 People call George Washington "The (Creator / Father) of His Country."

3 Americans wanted to build a (monument / temple) for George Washington.

4 Construction on the Washington Monument finished in (1884 / 1984).

5 The Washington Monument is a large (pyramid / obelisk) 555 feet high.

D Listen to the talk. Then, read a part of the talk and guess the meaning of the underlined word.

Notes

His armies had successfully conquered lands all over Europe. He wanted to create a monument in honor of those victories.

ⓐ battled
ⓑ taken over
ⓒ invaded

Unit 14 The Leaning Tower of Pisa

A Listen to the talk on page 70 again. Then, write the answers to the questions.

1 What was the original purpose of the Leaning Tower of Pisa?

____

2 Why did the builders construct the Leaning Tower of Pisa on unsuitable ground?

____

3 When did the first stage of construction end?

____

4 What have people tried to do to the Leaning Tower of Pisa over the centuries?

____

5 Why is the Leaning Tower of Pisa one of the most recognizable buildings in the world?

____

B Use the words in the box to complete the sentences.

inexperienced	lean	fall over	erect	unsuitable

1 The boxes will ______________ if you put too many on top of one another.

2 This campsite is very close to the river, so it is ______________.

3 He is ______________ at programming, so he will make a lot of mistakes.

4 Do not ______________ against the door because it might suddenly open.

5 How long will it take to ______________ the building?

C **Listen to the talk on page 72 again. Then, choose the correct answers.**

1 Eric is calling Mary from ________________, Italy.

ⓐ Venice ⓑ Rome ⓒ Florence

2 Eric's favorite place was the ________________.

ⓐ Colosseum ⓑ Vatican ⓒ Forum

3 There were four different ________________ in the stadium.

ⓐ seats ⓑ regions ⓒ levels

4 More than ________________ people could watch events at one time.

ⓐ 50,000 ⓑ 70,000 ⓒ 100,000

5 ________________ fought there while people watched.

ⓐ Emperors ⓑ Armies ⓒ Gladiators

D **Listen to the talk. Then, read a part of the talk and guess the meaning of the underlined word.**

Notes

> The ancient Romans were amazing builders. They excelled at engineering and used <u>advanced</u> construction methods, too.

ⓐ unknown
ⓑ inefficient
ⓒ superior

Unit 15 The Taj Mahal

A **Listen to the talk on page 74 again. Then, write the answers to the questions.**

1 Who was Mumtaz Mahal?

____

2 What did the Shah do when his wife died?

____

3 How many architects designed the Taj Mahal?

____

4 What does the name Taj Mahal mean in English?

____

5 What was used to make the Taj Mahal?

____

B **Use the words in the box to complete the sentences.**

was devastated	architect	labor	fitting	give birth to

1 Tim ______________ when his grandfather died of cancer.

2 The ______________ is designing a large office building.

3 Let's find a ______________ place to raise our family.

4 Mrs. Peters is going to ______________ twin boys.

5 They must ______________ very hard to finish the work on time.

C Listen to the talk on page 76 again. Then, fill in the blanks with the correct words.

1 The Sydney Opera House sits alongside ________________.

2 There are around 3,000 ________________ at the Sydney Opera House every year.

3 The Sydney Opera House has a unique ________________.

4 The opera house has many ________________ that are made of tile.

5 ________________ designed the Sydney Opera House.

D Listen to the talk. Then, match the sentences to complete the supporting details.

Notes

1 The official name — ⓐ more than 150 years old.

2 The clock — ⓑ of the clock is Clock Tower.

3 Big Ben is — ⓒ is a symbol of London.

Unit 16 The Statue of Liberty

A **Listen to the talk on page 78 again. Then, write the answers to the questions.**

1 Where is the Statue of Liberty?

____

2 Which country was an ally of the Americans during the Revolutionary War?

____

3 Who designed the Statue of Liberty?

____

4 What is the Statue of Liberty holding in her hands?

____

5 When was the Statue of Liberty dedicated?

____

B **Use the words in the box to complete the sentences.**

independence	torch	pedestal	ally	was dedicated

1 The monument ______________ to the people who died defending the city.

2 The people of that colony wanted their ______________ from Spain.

3 Thanks to the bright ______________, we can see in the dark cave.

4 The country's ______________ sent an army to help defend it from the invaders.

5 The statue is standing on a large marble ______________.

C Listen to the talk on page 80 again. Then, answer T (true) or F (false).

1 ______ Walter Schnell immigrated to the United States in 1938.

2 ______ Walter Schnell and his family came from Russia.

3 ______ Everyone visited Ellis Island first.

4 ______ Immigrants to the United States never went to Ellis Island.

5 ______ The people on the ship saw the Statue of Liberty.

D Listen to the talk. Then, write MI (main idea) or SD (supporting detail).

Notes

1 ______ Eero Saarinen won a contest and designed the St. Louis Arch.

2 ______ The St. Louis Arch was made to honor settlers who traveled to the west.

3 ______ The St. Louis Arch is 630 feet wide and 630 feet high.

Chapter 5

The Ocean

Unit 17

Coral Reefs

A Listen to the talk on page 84 again. Then, write the answers to the questions.

1 What kind of water can coral reefs survive in?

____

2 What percentage of all ocean animals live in or around coral reefs?

____

3 Where is the Great Barrier Reef?

____

4 Why can most large predators not swim in coral reefs?

____

5 Why do animals living in coral reefs have a constant supply of food?

____

B Use the words in the box to complete the sentences.

aquatic species	vital	evade	thrive	rich

1 It is ______________ that you succeed, or the plan will fail.

2 The wolves should ______________ in their new environment.

3 The land is ______________ in natural resources, so many people want to live there.

4 What kinds of ______________ live in this river?

5 The thieves are trying to ______________ the police right now.

C Listen to the talk on page 86 again. Then, circle the correct answers.

1 Hanauma Bay is on the island of (Oahu / Lanai).

2 Hanauma Bay is located in the crater of (an extinct / a dormant) volcano.

3 More than 450 species of tropical (mammals / fish) live there.

4 Hanauma Bay is a nature (preserve / reservation) now.

5 Tourists can swim in the reef, but they cannot go (snorkeling / fishing).

D Listen to the talk. Practice dictation by writing the exact words the speaker says.

Notes

1 In some places, ______________________________.

2 But they often ______________________________.

3 Coral is very sensitive, so it can't survive in ______________________.

Unit 18 The Mariana Trench

A **Listen to the talk on page 88 again. Then, write the answers to the questions.**

1 How deep is the Mariana Trench?

____

2 What was the name of the ship that discovered the deepest part of the trench?

____

3 Why could humans not explore the bottom of the trench for many years?

____

4 What do the vents in the trench do?

____

5 What lives at the bottom of the trench?

____

B **Use the words in the box to complete the sentences.**

valuable	an abundance of life	trench	descend	microbe

1 It is sometimes harder to ______________ a mountain than to climb it.

2 There is ______________ in the rainforest.

3 A ______________ is so small that you cannot see it unless you have a microscope.

4 Janet is a ______________ member of the club.

5 There is a deep ______________ in that part of the ocean.

C Listen to the talk on page 90 again. Then, choose the correct answers.

1 James Cameron ________________ the movies *Titanic* and *Avatar*.

ⓐ wrote ⓑ directed ⓒ acted in

2 James Cameron made a ________________ dive to the bottom of the Mariana Trench.

ⓐ solo ⓑ two-man ⓒ long-term

3 James Cameron used a deep-sea ________________ to go to the bottom of the trench.

ⓐ substance ⓑ submarine ⓒ submersible

4 James Cameron discovered some new ________________ of animals.

ⓐ versions ⓑ species ⓒ names

5 James Cameron is going to appear on the ________________.

ⓐ website ⓑ show ⓒ news

D Listen to the talk. Practice dictation by writing the exact words the speaker says.

Notes

1 First, scientists ____.

2 Animals such as ____.

3 Angler fish and flounder are just two of ____.

Unit 19 Deep-Sea Creatures

A Listen to the talk on page 92 again. Then, write the answers to the questions.

1 Where do oceans become very deep?

____

2 What is the water like deep beneath the surface?

____

3 What are living fossils?

____

4 What kind of animal is the frilled shark?

____

5 What does bioluminescence do for animals?

____

B Use the words in the box to complete the sentences.

water pressure	bioluminescence	barely	incredibly	harsh

1 The conditions in the prison are very _______________ for the prisoners.

2 The deeper underwater you go, the greater the _______________ becomes.

3 I am so tired that I can _______________ keep my eyes open.

4 The anglerfish uses _______________ to make its own light.

5 We were all surprised when Jim made an _______________ difficult shot.

C Listen to the talk on page 94 again. Then, fill in the blanks with the correct words.

1 Life exists in the hottest ________________ and in the coldest places on the Earth.

2 The stratosphere is one layer of the ________________.

3 Many ________________ live in the stratosphere.

4 Some bacteria, fungi, and viruses are very ________________ to humans.

5 ________________ do not know how microbes can live high in the stratosphere.

D Listen to the talk. Then, complete the classification chart about Arctic Ocean animals.

Notes

Arctic Ocean Animals

- Can be very ⓐ ________________
- Are mammals such as walruses, polar bears, and ⓑ ________________
- ⓒ ________________ layers of fat keep bodies warm
- Have thick ⓓ ________________
- Fur keeps cold water from ⓔ ________________ their bodies

Unit 20 Sharks

A **Listen to the talk on page 96 again. Then, write the answers to the questions.**

1 About how many shark attacks are there each year?

____

2 How many species of sharks are there?

____

3 What is the most fearsome creature in the ocean?

____

4 Where do tiger sharks live?

____

5 Where do bull sharks often swim?

____

B **Use the words in the box to complete the sentences.**

per	aggressive	is responsible for	man-eating shark	fearsome creature

1 Kevin ____________ the success of the project.

2 The diver saw a ____________ while he was swimming in the ocean.

3 The cost of the pizza is one dollar ____________ slice.

4 The giant squid is a ____________ that humans are afraid of.

5 Bears are sometimes ____________ and will attack humans.

C Listen to the talk on page 98 again. Then, answer T (true) or F (false).

1 ______ There was a shark attack near the beach.

2 ______ A large shark attacked a man swimming in the ocean.

3 ______ A man hit the shark in its eyes.

4 ______ A person should stay calm if he or she sees a shark.

5 ______ It is okay to try to swim faster than a shark.

D Listen to the talk. Then, complete the classification chart about the whale shark.

Notes

The Whale Shark

- Can be ⓐ ______________ meters long
- Can weigh more than twenty-three ⓑ ______________
- Has a ⓒ ______________ 1.5 meters wide
- Eats plankton and ⓓ ______________ fish
- Lets divers hold onto ⓔ ______________ and plays with some divers

memo

memo

Developing Listening Skills

2

DARAKWON

Table of Contents

Introduction

Developing Listening Skills Book 2 is the second book in a four-book series. This book is intended for elementary learners of the English language. By using this book, learners will be able to improve their listening skills as well as their knowledge of English.

Developing Listening Skills Book 2 contains twenty units. The twenty units are divided into five topics, each of which contains four units. The five topics in *Developing Listening Skills Book 2* are Amazing Places, Great Scientists, Historical Eras, Landmarks, and The Ocean. These are all topics that young learners find interesting and enjoy learning about. So learners will have fun listening to the material in this book while improving their English at the same time.

Every unit contains one main talk, a shorter talk, and questions about these talks. Each unit also contains a listening skill and exercises on it. The listening skills will help learners improve various aspects of their listening abilities.

Developing Listening Skills Book 2 has several objectives. First, it will help learners improve their English abilities, particularly their listening skills. Next, it will teach them valuable knowledge about a wide range of academic topics. The talks themselves will also entertain learners as they listen to them. Finally, *Developing Listening Skills Book 2* will help learners prepare for various standardized tests that they may take in the future. For instance, many questions about the talks are similar to those that appear on the iBT TOEFL® Junior and iBT TOEFL® exams. So, by using this book, learners should be able to get higher scores on the tests they take in the future.

About This Book

There are a total of twenty units. Each unit contains one main talk about a specific topic. There are vocabulary and listening comprehension questions about the main talk. There is also a shorter talk with listening comprehension questions. There are a total of ten listening skills that are taught in the various chapters. Finally, there is a comprehensive vocabulary section as well as a workbook that will help learners increase their understanding of the talks and improve their English abilities.

Unit 01 The Amazon Rainforest

Pre-Listening Questions

Answer the following questions.
1 Where is the Amazon Rainforest?
2 What kinds of animals live in the Amazon Rainforest?
3 What else do you know about the Amazon Rainforest?

Vocabulary

Look at the pictures. Write the correct word(s) from the box for each picture.

jungle floor canopy native Indian

Unit 01 11

Pre-Listening Questions

There are three questions that focus on the picture or pictures at the top of the page. These questions will help prepare learners for the topic of the unit.

Vocabulary

This section contains three vocabulary words from the main talk. Learners should match the words with the pictures.

Talk

This is the main talk of the unit. Each talk is around 220-250 words long and focuses on the topic of the unit.

Organizer

This is a graphic organizer of the talk. There are six blanks for learners to fill in by using words in the talk.

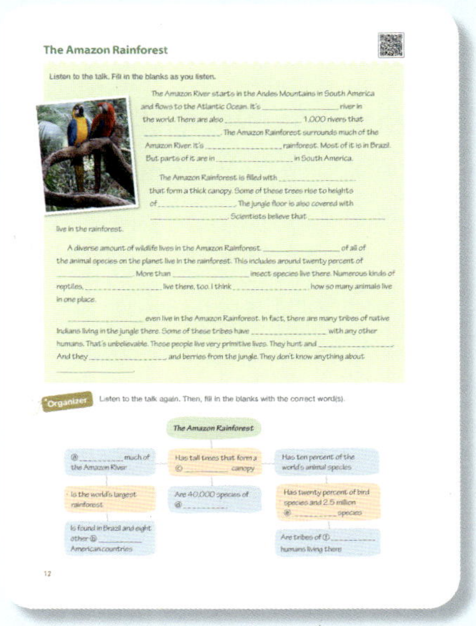
The Amazon Rainforest

Listen to the talk. Fill in the blanks as you listen.

Organizer Listen to the talk again. Then, fill in the blanks with the correct word(s).

The Amazon Rainforest

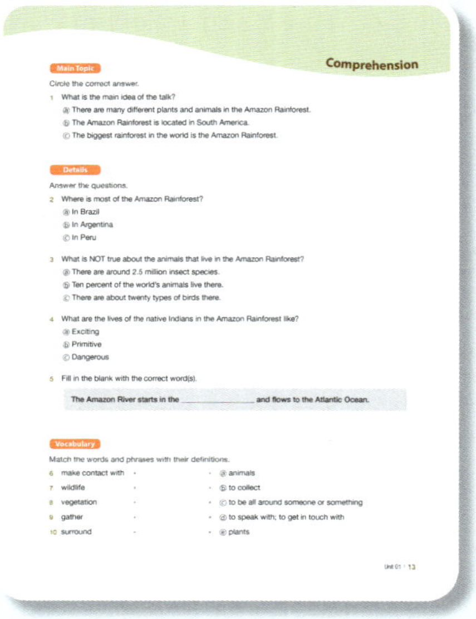
Comprehension

Main Topic

Circle the correct answer.

1 What is the main idea of the talk?
ⓐ There are many different plants and animals in the Amazon Rainforest.
ⓑ The Amazon Rainforest is located in South America.
ⓒ The biggest rainforest in the world is the Amazon Rainforest.

Details

Answer the questions.

2 Where is most of the Amazon Rainforest?
ⓐ In Brazil
ⓑ In Argentina
ⓒ In Peru

3 What is NOT true about the animals that live in the Amazon Rainforest?
ⓐ There are around 2.5 million insect species.
ⓑ Ten percent of the world's animals live there.
ⓒ There are about twenty types of birds there.

4 What are the lives of the native Indians in the Amazon Rainforest like?
ⓐ Exciting
ⓑ Primitive
ⓒ Dangerous

5 Fill in the blank with the correct word(s).

The Amazon River starts in the ________ and flows to the Atlantic Ocean.

Vocabulary

Match the words and phrases with their definitions.

6 make contact with • • ⓐ animals
7 wildlife • • ⓑ to collect
8 vegetation • • ⓒ to be all around someone or something
9 gather • • ⓓ to speak with; to get in touch with
10 surround • • ⓔ plants

Unit 01 13

Comprehension

This page contains several questions about the main talk. There is a question about the main topic or main idea of the talk. There are also four questions that ask about the details in the talk. Finally, there are five vocabulary questions for learners to test their knowledge of the words in the talk.

Listening Skills Practice

This section provides further practice for learners. First, there is a listening skills section in each unit. Various listening skills, such as detail, chronological order, note-taking, dictation, and outlining, are covered in each unit. There is a description of the listening skill as well as questions for learners to test their understanding of the listening skill.

In addition, there is a short talk that is around 140-160 words long. Each talk provides information about a topic related to the main talk. There are comprehension questions and listening skill questions for each short talk as well.

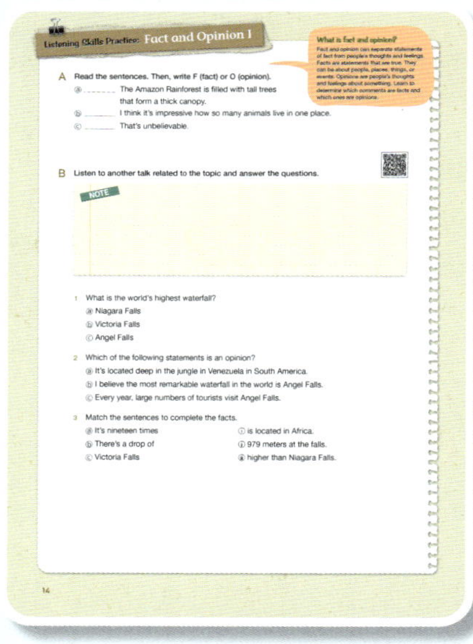
Listening Skills Practice Fact and Opinion I

What is fact and opinion?

A Read the sentences. Then, write F (fact) or O (opinion).
ⓐ ______ The Amazon Rainforest is filled with tall trees that form a thick canopy.
ⓑ ______ I think it's impressive how so many animals live in one place.
ⓒ ______ That's unbelievable.

B Listen to another talk related to the topic and answer the questions.

NOTE

1 What is the world's highest waterfall?
ⓐ Niagara Falls
ⓑ Victoria Falls
ⓒ Angel Falls

2 Which of the following statements is an opinion?
ⓐ It's located deep in the jungle in Venezuela in South America.
ⓑ I believe the most remarkable waterfall in the world is Angel Falls.
ⓒ Every year, large numbers of tourists visit Angel Falls.

3 Match the sentences to complete the facts.
ⓐ It's nineteen times ⓓ is located in Africa.
ⓑ There's a drop of ⓔ 979 meters at the falls.
ⓒ Victoria Falls ⓕ higher than Niagara Falls.

14

Chapter 1

Amazing Places

Unit 01

The Amazon Rainforest

Pre-Listening Questions

Answer the following questions.

1 Where is the Amazon Rainforest?

2 What kinds of animals live in the Amazon Rainforest?

3 What else do you know about the Amazon Rainforest?

Vocabulary

Look at the pictures. Write the correct word(s) from the box for each picture.

jungle floor	canopy	native Indian

1 
______

2 
______

3 
______

The Amazon Rainforest

Listen to the talk. Fill in the blanks as you listen.

The Amazon River starts in the Andes Mountains in South America and flows to the Atlantic Ocean. It's __________ river in the world. There are also __________ 1,000 rivers that __________. The Amazon Rainforest surrounds much of the Amazon River. It's __________ rainforest. Most of it is in Brazil. But parts of it are in __________ in South America.

The Amazon Rainforest is filled with __________ that form a thick canopy. Some of these trees rise to heights of __________. The jungle floor is also covered with __________. Scientists believe that __________ live in the rainforest.

A diverse amount of wildlife lives in the Amazon Rainforest. __________ of all of the animal species on the planet live in the rainforest. This includes around twenty percent of __________. More than __________ insect species live there. Numerous kinds of reptiles, __________ live there, too. I think __________ how so many animals live in one place.

__________ even live in the Amazon Rainforest. In fact, there are many tribes of native Indians living in the jungle there. Some of these tribes have __________ with any other humans. That's unbelievable. These people live very primitive lives. They hunt and __________. And they __________, and berries from the jungle. They don't know anything about __________.

Organizer Listen to the talk again. Then, fill in the blanks with the correct word(s).

The Amazon Rainforest

- ⓐ __________ much of the Amazon River
- Is the world's largest rainforest
- Is found in Brazil and eight other ⓑ __________ American countries
- Has tall trees that form a ⓒ __________ canopy
- Are 40,000 species of ⓓ __________
- Has ten percent of the world's animal species
- Has twenty percent of bird species and 2.5 million ⓔ __________ species
- Are tribes of ⓕ __________ humans living there

Comprehension

Main Topic

Circle the correct answer.

1 What is the main idea of the talk?

ⓐ There are many different plants and animals in the Amazon Rainforest.

ⓑ The Amazon Rainforest is located in South America.

ⓒ The biggest rainforest in the world is the Amazon Rainforest.

Details

Answer the questions.

2 Where is most of the Amazon Rainforest?

ⓐ In Brazil

ⓑ In Argentina

ⓒ In Peru

3 What is NOT true about the animals that live in the Amazon Rainforest?

ⓐ There are around 2.5 million insect species.

ⓑ Ten percent of the world's animals live there.

ⓒ There are about twenty types of birds there.

4 What are the lives of the native Indians in the Amazon Rainforest like?

ⓐ Exciting

ⓑ Primitive

ⓒ Dangerous

5 Fill in the blank with the correct word(s).

The Amazon River starts in the ________________ and flows to the Atlantic Ocean.

Vocabulary

Match the words and phrases with their definitions.

6 make contact with	•	• ⓐ animals
7 wildlife	•	• ⓑ to collect
8 vegetation	•	• ⓒ to be all around someone or something
9 gather	•	• ⓓ to speak with; to get in touch with
10 surround	•	• ⓔ plants

Listening Skills Practice: Fact and Opinion I

What is fact and opinion?

Fact and opinion can separate statements of fact from people's thoughts and feelings. Facts are statements that are true. They can be about people, places, things, or events. Opinions are people's thoughts and feelings about something. Learn to determine which comments are facts and which ones are opinions.

A Read the sentences. Then, write F (fact) or O (opinion).

ⓐ ________ The Amazon Rainforest is filled with tall trees that form a thick canopy.

ⓑ ________ I think it's impressive how so many animals live in one place.

ⓒ ________ That's unbelievable.

B Listen to another talk related to the topic and answer the questions.

NOTE

1 What is the world's highest waterfall?

ⓐ Niagara Falls

ⓑ Victoria Falls

ⓒ Angel Falls

2 Which of the following statements is an opinion?

ⓐ It's located deep in the jungle in Venezuela in South America.

ⓑ I believe the most remarkable waterfall in the world is Angel Falls.

ⓒ Every year, large numbers of tourists visit Angel Falls.

3 Match the sentences to complete the facts.

ⓐ It's nineteen times	ⓘ is located in Africa.
ⓑ There's a drop of	ⓘⓘ 979 meters at the falls.
ⓒ Victoria Falls	ⓘⓘⓘ higher than Niagara Falls.

Unit **02**

The Grand Canyon

Pre-Listening Questions

Answer the following questions.

1 Where is the Grand Canyon?

2 How did the Grand Canyon form?

3 Do you know how old the Grand Canyon is?

Vocabulary

Look at the pictures. Write the correct word(s) from the box for each picture.

rafting	hike	canyon

1  ______________

2  ______________

3  ______________

The Grand Canyon

Listen to the talk. Fill in the blanks as you listen.

The Colorado River ____________ the southwestern part of the United States. Millions of years ago, the land it flowed through ____________. Then, the river slowly began eroding the land. Over time, it ____________ large amounts of land. A canyon then formed. Today, we know it as the Grand Canyon. It's one of the ____________ of the world. And it's a place I believe everyone should visit ____________. You will love the Grand Canyon if you go there.

The Grand Canyon ____________ the American state of Arizona. It's nearly 500 kilometers long. It's more than ____________ in many places. And it's around twenty-nine kilometers wide in some places. ____________ of the canyon, the Colorado River still flows through it ____________ to the Gulf of California.

In the past, many ____________ lived in the Grand Canyon. Today, only a few Native Americans live there. But the entire Grand Canyon is now a national park. So it's ____________. More than five million visitors from around the world visit the Grand Canyon each year. Most of them stay on ____________. The northern rim gets fewer visitors. I think the northern rim has ____________ than the southern rim though. The majority of tourists stay at the top of the Grand Canyon. A few hike all the way to the bottom. And some even ____________ through the Grand Canyon.

Organizer Listen to the talk again. Then, fill in the blanks with the correct word(s).

The Grand Canyon

- ⓐ ____________ millions of years ago
  - Was created due to ⓑ ____________ caused by the Colorado River
- Is located in Arizona, USA
  - Is almost 500 kilometers long
  - Is 1,800 meters deep and 29 kilometers ⓒ ____________ in some places
- Is a ⓓ ____________ park
  - Gets about 5 million ⓔ ____________ per year
  - Some ⓕ ____________ to the bottom or go rafting through the Grand Canyon

Comprehension

Main Topic

Circle the correct answer.

1 What is the main topic of the talk?

ⓐ Some facts about the Grand Canyon

ⓑ Why people should visit the Grand Canyon

ⓒ How to get to the Grand Canyon

Details

Answer the questions.

2 What formed the Grand Canyon?

ⓐ The Colorado River

ⓑ Wind erosion

ⓒ Earthquakes

3 Which of the following is NOT true about the Grand Canyon?

ⓐ It is around 500 kilometers long.

ⓑ It is more than 1,800 kilometers deep in some places.

ⓒ It is around 29 kilometers wide in a few areas.

4 What is the teacher's opinion of the views at the Grand Canyon?

ⓐ There are no better views in the world.

ⓑ They are better from the bottom.

ⓒ They are better at the northern rim.

5 Fill in the blank with the correct word(s).

The Grand Canyon formed ________________ of years ago because of water erosion.

Vocabulary

Match the words and phrases with their definitions.

6	rim	ⓐ to wear down over time
7	majority	ⓑ a group of people who are similar or the same
8	erode	ⓒ a place that is kept safe
9	protected area	ⓓ the most; the greatest number
10	tribe	ⓔ the edge or outer part of something

Listening Skills Practice: Fact and Opinion II

What is fact and opinion?

Fact and opinion can separate statements of fact from people's thoughts and feelings. Facts are details in a talk. They are true statements about people, places, things, or events. People often state their opinions about facts. They frequently use the words *think*, *believe*, and *feel* to give their opinions.

A Read the sentences. Then, write F (fact) or O (opinion).

ⓐ ________ You will love the Grand Canyon if you go there.

ⓑ ________ In the past, many Native American tribes lived in the Grand Canyon.

ⓒ ________ I think the northern rim has better views than the southern rim though.

B Listen to a talk by a tour guide related to the topic and answer the questions.

Memo

1 What are the people going to see during their trip?

ⓐ Rapids on the water

ⓑ Some Indian ruins

ⓒ A lot of unique wildlife

2 Which of the following statements is an opinion?

ⓐ We're going to go rafting down the Colorado River.

ⓑ You're going to get a view of the Grand Canyon that few people ever experience.

ⓒ The ruins are fascinating.

3 Match the sentences to complete the facts.

ⓐ There won't be	ⓘ go rafting down the Colorado River.
ⓑ We're going to have	ⓘⓘ any rapids.
ⓒ We're going to	ⓘⓘⓘ lunch at the bottom of the canyon.

Unit 03

The Serengeti

Pre-Listening Questions

Answer the following questions.

1 Where is the Serengeti?

2 What animals can you see in the pictures?

3 What do you think life is like in the Serengeti?

Vocabulary

Look at the pictures. Write the correct word(s) from the box for each picture.

wildebeest	plain	hyena

1 

____

2 

____

3 

____

The Serengeti

Listen to the talk. Fill in the blanks as you listen.

Africa is the world's second largest continent. It has an interesting geography. For instance, there are ____________________ in the north. In the central region, there are rainforests. And in the eastern part of the continent, there is ____________________. This area is ____________________ people call it Siringitu. That means "endless plain." The English word Serengeti ____________________.

The Serengeti is located in Tanzania and Kenya. It covers an area of around ____________________ kilometers. Most of the Serengeti is ____________________. There are some wooded areas, wetlands, and ____________________. Yet the land is ____________________ few trees for as far as the eye can see.

The Serengeti is teeming with wildlife. In fact, some of the largest land animals on the planet live there. ____________________ of elephants, hippopotamuses, giraffes, and rhinoceroses live there. Yet their numbers are ____________________ with ____________________ of other animals that live in the Serengeti. There are herds of zebras, wildebeests, gazelles, and buffalos that ____________________ thousands of animals.

There are also large numbers of predators in the Serengeti. ____________________ such as lions, leopards, and cheetahs prowl the land. Hyenas and jackals live there ____________________. The rivers and lakes ____________________ vicious crocodiles. There are all kinds of smaller predators as well. They spend much of their time ____________________ animals that live in the Serengeti.

Organizer Listen to the talk again. Then, fill in the blanks with the correct word(s).

The Serengeti

- Is a vast plain located in eastern ⓐ ____________
- Is located in Tanzania and ⓑ ____________
- Is mostly flat grasslands

- Has very large animals such as elephants, hippos, ⓒ ____________, and rhinos
- Has huge herds of zebras, wildebeests, gazelles, and buffalos
- Are many ⓓ ____________ there
  - Are great cats such as ⓔ ____________, leopards, and cheetahs
  - Are hyenas, jackals, and ⓕ ____________

Comprehension

Main Topic

Circle the correct answer.

1 What is the main idea of the talk?

ⓐ The geography of Africa includes deserts, rainforests, and plains.

ⓑ There are many types of animals that live in the Serengeti.

ⓒ The Serengeti is a vast plain located in Kenya and Tanzania.

Details

Answer the questions.

2 What does Siringitu mean?

ⓐ Very hot desert

ⓑ Giant rainforest

ⓒ Endless plain

3 Which country is the Serengeti NOT in?

ⓐ Kenya

ⓑ Egypt

ⓒ Tanzania

4 Which animals live in herds of hundreds of thousands in the Serengeti?

ⓐ Zebras

ⓑ Elephants

ⓒ Hippopotamuses

5 Fill in the blank with the correct word(s).

There are many ____________________ in the Serengeti, including lions, cheetahs, leopards, and crocodiles.

Vocabulary

Match the words and phrases with their definitions.

6	wooded area	ⓐ wide; extensive; very big
7	herd	ⓑ to have a large number of
8	vast	ⓒ a forest; a region with many trees
9	be teeming with	ⓓ to move slowly and silently to hunt other animals
10	prowl	ⓔ a large group of animals

Listening Skills Practice: Paraphrasing I

What is paraphrasing?

Paraphrasing is a way to simplify a long talk. Sometimes a talk may be long and confusing. To paraphrase, omit the unimportant information. Focus only on the important information in the talk. Then, make a sentence that contains all of the important information. You can paraphrase a single sentence or many sentences together.

A Read a part of the talk. Then, choose the correct paraphrase.

> The Serengeti is located in Tanzania and Kenya. It covers an area of around 30,000 square kilometers. Most the Serengeti is flat grassland. There are some wooded areas, wetlands, and hilly areas. Yet the land is mostly flat with few trees for as far as the eye can see.

ⓐ The Serengeti is a huge flat grassland in Tanzania and Kenya.
ⓑ There are a few trees and hills located in the Serengeti.
ⓒ Even though the Serengeti is large, it is only in two countries.

B Listen to another talk related to the topic and answer the questions.

NOTE

1 Why do animals migrate to new lands in the Great Migration?
ⓐ To escape from other animals
ⓑ To find food to eat
ⓒ To give birth to their young

2 What is in the rivers that the animals must cross?
ⓐ Crocodiles
ⓑ Hippopotamuses
ⓒ Snakes

3 Read a part of the talk. Then, choose the correct paraphrase.

> The Great Migration involves more than two million large herbivores. There are more than one million wildebeests. Large herds of zebras, gazelles, and other animals migrate as well.

ⓐ There are many zebras, gazelles, and other animals living in the Serengeti.
ⓑ More than two million animals, include wildebeests, zebras, and gazelles, join the Great Migration.
ⓒ Both herbivores and carnivores join the Great Migration.

Unit 04 The Dead Sea

Pre-Listening Questions

Answer the following questions.

1 Where is the Dead Sea?

2 What is the person doing in the water?

3 What do you know about the Dead Sea?

Vocabulary

Look at the pictures. Write the correct word(s) from the box for each picture.

float	plateau	surface

1 

____

2 

____

3 

____

The Dead Sea

Listen to the talk. Fill in the blanks as you listen.

One of the most unique places in the world is found ____________ between Israel and Jordan in the Middle East. It's the Dead Sea. The Dead Sea ____________ plateaus east and west of it. The Jordan River flows into it ____________. And some small streams flow into it in from the east. The Dead Sea is around ____________ and eighteen kilometers wide at some points.

The Dead Sea ____________. It's a very large lake. But it has a number of characteristics that ____________. First, it's the lowest place on the Earth. The surface of the Dead Sea is more than 400 meters ____________. In addition, ____________ or plants live in the Dead Sea. Sometimes fish swim into the Dead Sea from the Jordan River or various streams. They ____________.

The reason is that the Dead Sea has a very ____________. Water flows into the Dead Sea. But no water flows out. Over time, some of the water evaporates. But the salt and ____________. The salt content in some parts of the Dead Sea is about ____________. This means that thirty-five percent of the water is really salt. It's so salty that people can ____________ the water of the Dead Sea. Many people even visit the Dead Sea because of the salt water. They claim ____________ all sorts of physical problems.

Organizer Listen to the talk again. Then, fill in the blanks with the correct word(s).

The Dead Sea

- Is on the ⓐ ________ of Israel and Jordan
- Is between plateaus to the east and west
- Has the Jordan River and ⓑ ________ flowing into it
- Is 80 kilometers long and up to ⓒ ________ kilometers wide

- Is not a sea but a very large ⓓ ________
- Is the ⓔ ________ place on the Earth
- Has no fish or plants living in it because of its high salt content
- Is so ⓕ ________ that people can easily float on the water's surface

Comprehension

Main Topic

Circle the correct answer.

1 What is the main topic of the talk?

ⓐ Some features of the Dead Sea

ⓑ The popularity of the Dead Sea

ⓒ The way the Dead Sea formed

Details

Answer the questions.

2 Which country is the Dead Sea NOT located in?

ⓐ Israel

ⓑ Syria

ⓒ Jordan

3 Which statement about the Dead Sea is true?

ⓐ Its surface is 400 meters below sea level.

ⓑ It is located between some tall mountains.

ⓒ It has a wide variety of fish living in it.

4 Why can people easily float on the Dead Sea?

ⓐ The low altitude of the sea lets them float.

ⓑ There is very much oxygen in the water.

ⓒ The water has a high salt content.

5 Fill in the blank with the correct word(s).

Many people believe that the salt water in the Dead Sea can heal their ________________.

Vocabulary

Match the words and phrases with their definitions.

6 notable	ⓐ the amount of salt in a substance
7 evaporate	ⓑ to change from a solid or liquid to a gas
8 sea level	ⓒ the line that separates one country from another
9 salt content	ⓓ famous; well-known; remarkable
10 border	ⓔ the average level of the surface of the sea

Listening Skills Practice: Paraphrasing II

What is paraphrasing?

Paraphrasing is a way to simplify a long talk. Sometimes a talk may be very long. To paraphrase, omit the unimportant information. Focus only on the important information in the talk. Then, make one sentence with all of the important facts from the talk. Paraphrasing can help you remember the important parts of a talk.

A Read a part of the talk. Then, choose the correct paraphrase.

The Dead Sea actually isn't a sea. It's a very large lake. But it has a number of characteristics that make it notable. First, it's the lowest place on the Earth. The surface of the Dead Sea is more than 400 meters below sea level.

ⓐ The Dead Sea is only about 400 meters long, but it is far below the Earth's surface.
ⓑ Some people think that the Dead Sea is a sea, but it is actually just a lake.
ⓒ The Dead Sea is a large lake that is the lowest place on the Earth's surface.

B Listen to a talk by a tour guide related to the topic and answer the questions.

Memo

1 Where is the Great Blue Hole near?
ⓐ Bolivia
ⓑ Bulgaria
ⓒ Belize

2 What are the people going to do first?
ⓐ Visit the Great Blue Hole
ⓑ Go scuba diving
ⓒ Do some snorkeling

3 Read a part of the talk. Then, choose the correct paraphrase.

The Great Blue Hole is more than 300 meters in diameter. It forms a nearly perfect circle. But that's not the best part. It's an underwater sinkhole, so it goes down to a depth of more than 120 meters.

ⓐ The Great Blue Hole forms a nearly perfect circle that is 120 meters in diameter.
ⓑ The Great Blue Hole is an underwater sinkhole 300 meters in diameter and 120 meters deep.
ⓒ The Great Blue Hole descends more than 300 meters as it forms a perfect circle.

Chapter 2

Great Scientists

Unit 05

Hippocrates

Pre-Listening Questions

Answer the following questions.

1 What is the doctor in the picture doing?

2 Who was Hippocrates?

3 How did Hippocrates affect modern-day doctors?

Vocabulary

Look at the pictures. Write the correct word(s) from the box for each picture.

graduate	sickness	observation

1 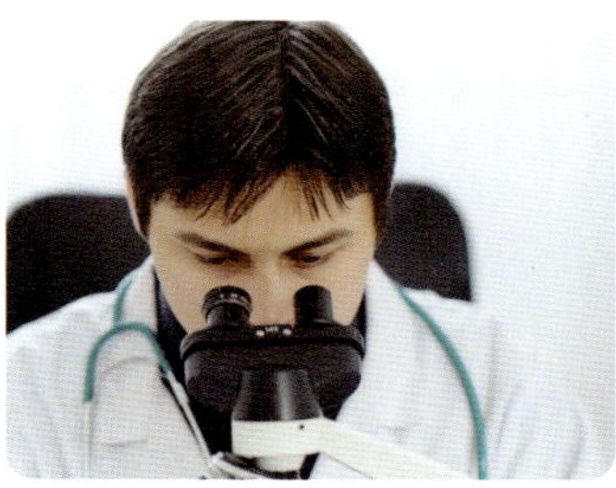

____

2 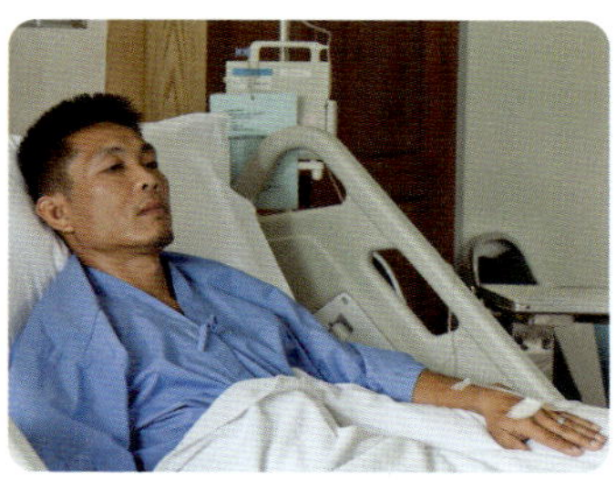

____

3 

____

Hippocrates

Listen to the talk. Fill in the blanks as you listen.

Thousands of years ago, ____________________ why people got sick. ____________________ their illnesses on various gods and goddesses. They believed that deities got upset and ____________________. In addition, many people ____________________ minor illnesses. Around thirty percent of all babies died before they were a year old. And most people only lived until they were ____________________.

Yet one man didn't ____________________ about how people got sick. Instead, he ____________________ on medicine ____________________ sick people. This man was Hippocrates. He was a Greek from the island of Cos. He was born around 460 B.C. And he passed away around 377 B.C.

During Hippocrates's long life, he had a tremendous affect on the ____________________. In fact, people call him "the father of modern medicine." He transformed the study of medicine from a field ____________________ to one based on observation. He thought that sicknesses and diseases had ____________________. So he tried to figure them out. Hippocrates learned ____________________ several diseases. And he made sure to write down everything that he learned. In that way, he ____________________ with others. Thanks to him, the Greeks learned a great deal about medical science.

Even today, ____________________ Hippocrates. When most doctors graduate from medical school, they take the Hippocratic Oath. They promise to ____________________ to their patients and to ____________________ to the best of their ability.

Organizer Listen to the talk again. Then, fill in the blanks with the correct word(s).

Ancient Beliefs

- Illnesses blamed on ⓐ ____________ and goddesses
- Thought deities were upset so made people sick
- Many ⓑ ____________ died, and most people only lived until they were in their 40s
- People often died from minor illnesses

Hippocrates

- Was a Greek who lived from ⓒ ____________ to 377 B.C.
- Was called "the ⓓ ____________ of medicine"
- Doctors take the Hippocratic Oath today and promise to do no ⓔ ____________
- Thought that sicknesses and ⓕ ____________ had natural causes

Comprehension

Main Topic

Circle the correct answer.

1 What is the main topic of the talk?

ⓐ Greece during the life of Hippocrates

ⓑ The greatest doctor in the history of medicine

ⓒ How Hippocrates changed the study of medicine

Details

Answer the questions.

2 Thousands of years ago, why did people think they became sick?

ⓐ Germs caused their bodies to become weak.

ⓑ The gods were upset with them.

ⓒ They did not eat the proper foods.

3 How did Hippocrates study medicine?

ⓐ Through observation

ⓑ Through experimentation

ⓒ Through superstition

4 According to the talk, what did Hippocrates NOT do?

ⓐ He learned that sicknesses had natural causes.

ⓑ He wrote down what he learned about medicine.

ⓒ He founded the first medical school in Greece.

5 Fill in the blank with the correct word(s).

Today, doctors say the ________________ when they graduate from medical school.

Vocabulary

Match the words and phrases with their definitions.

6	deity	ⓐ a god or goddess
7	based on	ⓑ to die
8	transform	ⓒ a belief that is not dependent on logic or knowledge
9	pass away	ⓓ to change
10	superstition	ⓔ depending on; relying on

Listening Skills Practice: Details I

What are details?
Details are the facts in a talk. There are many kinds of details. Details include names, dates, and places. They are explanations of the actions people do. They are also facts about people's lives.

A Write the correct details in the blanks.

ⓐ In the past, people died of minor ________________,
and many ________________ died before they were one year old.

ⓑ People often called ________________ "the father of modern ________________."

ⓒ Hippocrates learned how to treat several ________________, and he ________________ down everything he learned.

B Listen to another talk related to the topic and answer the questions.

NOTE

1 Where did Galen go to study medicine?
ⓐ Athens
ⓑ Alexandria
ⓒ Rome

2 What is theriac?
ⓐ A kind of medicine
ⓑ A type of surgery
ⓒ A part of the body

3 Write T (true) or F (false) for the following statements about Galen.
ⓐ ________ He was Greek, but he lived in Rome.
ⓑ ________ He fought as a gladiator in Roman arenas.
ⓒ ________ He became the personal doctor for Emperor Marcus Aurelius.

Unit 06

Nicholas Copernicus

Pre-Listening Questions

Answer the following questions.

1 Who is this man in the picture?

2 When did Nicholas Copernicus live?

3 What do you know about Nicholas Copernicus?

Vocabulary

Look at the pictures. Write the correct word(s) from the box for each picture.

orbit	solar system	Earth

1 

____

2 

____

3 

____

Nicholas Copernicus

Listen to the talk. Fill in the blanks as you listen.

People in the past __________ the sun, moon, stars, and planets. The ancient Egyptians and Chinese studied them. So did people in other cultures. For example, the ancient Greeks __________. The great philosopher Aristotle wrote __________. He believed Earth was __________ the universe. He thought that everything else—the sun, moon, stars, and planets—__________. This was the geocentric model of the universe.

For centuries, most people thought Aristotle's version of the universe __________. Then, Nicholas Copernicus began to study astronomy. He __________ to 1543. He lived in the middle of the Renaissance. It was __________. People at that time were especially interested in knowledge __________.

Copernicus read the works of Aristotle. Then, he __________ mathematical calculations for __________ of the stars. Copernicus was __________. But he couldn't get the __________ for Aristotle's model of the universe.

Copernicus __________ that Aristotle had been wrong. So he made his own model of the universe. In his model, __________ was at the center of the solar system. Earth was __________ from the sun. The __________. He put the other known planets—Mercury, Venus, Mars, Jupiter, and Saturn—in their correct orbits. This was the heliocentric model of the universe. Copernicus __________ in his book *On the Revolutions of Heavenly Bodies* just before he died.

Organizer Listen to the talk again. Then, fill in the blanks with the correct word(s).

The Geocentric Model of the Universe

- Was believed in by ⓐ __________
- Made Earth the ⓑ __________ of the universe
- Claimed that the sun, moon, stars, and planets orbited ⓒ __________

The Heliocentric Model of the Universe

- Was proposed by ⓓ __________
- Made the sun the center of the ⓔ __________
- Put the other planets in their ⓕ __________ orbits
- Earth was the third planet from the sun

Comprehension

Main Topic

Circle the correct answer.

1 What is the main idea of the talk?

ⓐ Nicholas Copernicus came up with the correct model of the universe.

ⓑ People used to believe in the geocentric model of the universe.

ⓒ The heliocentric model of the universe is the correct one.

Details

Answer the questions.

2 What was Aristotle's model of the universe called?

ⓐ The geocentric model

ⓑ The lunar-centric model

ⓒ The heliocentric model

3 When did Nicholas Copernicus live?

ⓐ During the time of ancient Greece

ⓑ During the Middle Ages

ⓒ During the Renaissance

4 What is NOT true about Nicholas Copernicus's model of the universe?

ⓐ It made Earth the third planet from the sun.

ⓑ It made the sun the center of the solar system.

ⓒ It contained all eight planets in the solar system.

5 Fill in the blank with the correct word(s).

Nicholas Copernicus studied astronomy and came up with the ________________ of the universe.

Vocabulary

Match the words and phrases with their definitions.

6	heliocentric	ⓐ an answer; the answer to a problem
7	calculation	ⓑ the study of the stars and planets
8	geocentric	ⓒ to be very interested in
9	be fascinated by	ⓓ having the sun at the center
10	astronomy	ⓔ having the Earth at the center

Listening Skills Practice: Details II

What are details?

Details are the facts in a talk. There are many kinds of details. Details provide more information about the events in a talk. They often answer questions that begin with wh-question words such as *who*, *what*, *when*, *where*, *how*, and *why*.

A **Write the correct details in the blanks.**

ⓐ The ancient Egyptians, ________________, and Greeks all studied ________________ in the past.

ⓑ ________________ tried to do the mathematical calculations for Aristotle's model of the ________________, but he was not successful.

ⓒ In the ________________ of the universe, the sun was at the center, and ________________ was the third planet from the sun.

B **Listen to a talk by a director of an observatory related to the topic and answer the questions.**

Memo

1 What is an ellipse?

ⓐ A shape like a square

ⓑ A shape like an oval

ⓒ A shape like a triangle

2 What was one of the laws of planetary motion that Johannes Kepler discovered?

ⓐ All of the planets orbit the sun at the same speed.

ⓑ All of the planets orbit the sun in an ellipse.

ⓒ All of the planets take years to move around the sun.

3 Write T (true) or F (false) for the following statements about Johannes Kepler.

ⓐ ________ He was a German astronomer.

ⓑ ________ He studied the orbit of Mercury.

ⓒ ________ He learned that the planets orbit the sun in a circle.

Unit 07

Albert Einstein

Pre-Listening Questions

Answer the following questions.

1 Who was Albert Einstein?

2 Why is he famous?

3 What other scientists do you know? What did they do?

Vocabulary

Look at the pictures. Write the correct word(s) from the box for each picture.

Nobel Prize	equation	professor

1 

____

2 

____

3 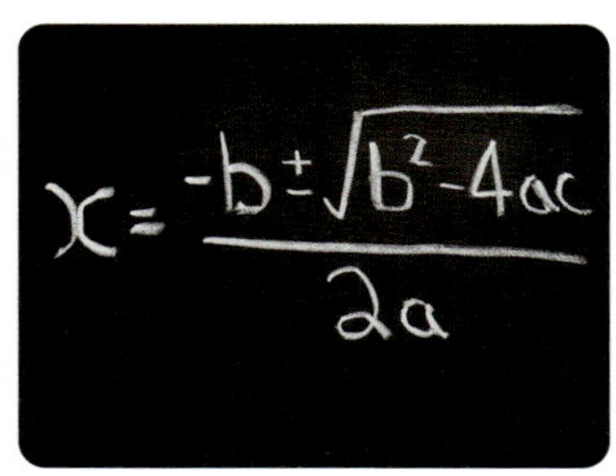

____

Albert Einstein

Listen to the talk. Fill in the blanks as you listen.

On March 14, 1879, Albert Einstein was born. He would become one of the greatest ______________. When he was young, his teachers didn't believe ______________. In fact, he was just ______________. Einstein didn't enjoy many of the subjects he studied. But he ______________ and math a lot.

Einstein ______________ school when he was fifteen. Later, he continued his studies. He finished his degree in 1900. Then, he ______________ working at the patent office in Bern, Switzerland. During his free time, he studied physics. In 1905, he published ______________. They were some of the most important scientific papers of the 1900s.

One of the papers concerned special relativity. The other contained ______________ $E = mc^2$. The equation describes how matter can be ______________. Thanks to those papers, people ______________ about Einstein. In 1910, he ______________ at the University of Zurich. ______________, he moved to Berlin, Germany and took a job there.

In 1919, Einstein's theory of relativity was proven ______________. This made him famous all around the world. ______________, he received the Nobel Prize in Physics. He continued to work in Germany. But he left the country ______________ the political situation in 1932. He moved to the United States and started working there. He continued to do ______________ until he died on April 18, 1955.

Organizer Listen to the talk again. Then, fill in the blanks with the correct word(s).

Albert Einstein

- Was born in 1879
- Didn't like all school ⓐ __________ but enjoyed science and math
- Worked in the ⓑ __________ office in Bern
- Published papers on special relativity and the equation $E = mc^2$ in 1905
- Theory of relativity proven ⓒ __________ in 1919
- Received the Nobel Prize in ⓓ __________ in 1921
- Left ⓔ __________ and went to the U.S. in 1932
- ⓕ __________ on April 18, 1955

Comprehension

Main Topic

Circle the correct answer.

1 What is the main topic of the talk?

ⓐ The life of Albert Einstein

ⓑ The research of Albert Einstein

ⓒ The Nobel Prize won by Albert Einstein

Details

Answer the questions.

2 What subject did Albert Einstein NOT enjoy at school?

ⓐ Math

ⓑ Literature

ⓒ Science

3 What was the equation that Albert Einstein wrote about in a paper in 1905?

ⓐ $a^2 + b^2 = c^2$

ⓑ $F = MA$

ⓒ $E = mc^2$

4 What happened to Albert Einstein in 1921?

ⓐ He became a professor in Berlin.

ⓑ He won the Nobel Prize in Physics.

ⓒ He moved to the United States.

5 Fill in the blank with the correct word(s).

Albert Einstein was one of the greatest ______________ in history.

Vocabulary

Match the words and phrases with their definitions.

6	theory	ⓐ to quit doing something
7	drop out of	ⓑ leisure time; time in which one has no work to do
8	free time	ⓒ material
9	average	ⓓ an idea; a hypothesis
10	matter	ⓔ normal; neither good nor bad

Listening Skills Practice: Sequencing I

What is sequencing?

Sequencing involves putting the events in a talk in the correct order. Begin with the first event. Then, continue by putting all of the events in the same order the speaker mentions them. Many speakers use dates when they speak. Listen carefully for the days, months, and years the speakers mention.

A **Listen to the talk again. Then, put the sentences in the correct order.**

ⓐ ________ Albert Einstein went to work at the patent office in Bern, Switzerland.

ⓑ ________ Albert Einstein left Germany because of the political situation.

ⓒ ________ Albert Einstein published a paper on special relativity.

B **Listen to another talk related to the topic and answer the questions.**

NOTE

1 What happened in 1939?

ⓐ The Manhattan Project began.

ⓑ Germany invaded Poland.

ⓒ The Americans made an atomic bomb.

2 Which person did NOT work on the Manhattan Project?

ⓐ Franklin Roosevelt

ⓑ Richard Feynman

ⓒ Robert Oppenheimer

3 Put the following sentences in the correct order.

ⓐ ________ The Manhattan Project began in 1941.

ⓑ ________ The Americans detonated the world's first atomic bomb.

ⓒ ________ Albert Einstein wrote a letter to President Roosevelt.

Unit 08

Marie Curie

Pre-Listening Questions

Answer the following questions.

1 What did Marie Curie do?

2 When did she live?

3 What else do you know about her life?

Vocabulary

Look at the pictures. Write the correct word(s) from the box for each picture.

X-ray machine	research project	treatment

1 

____

2 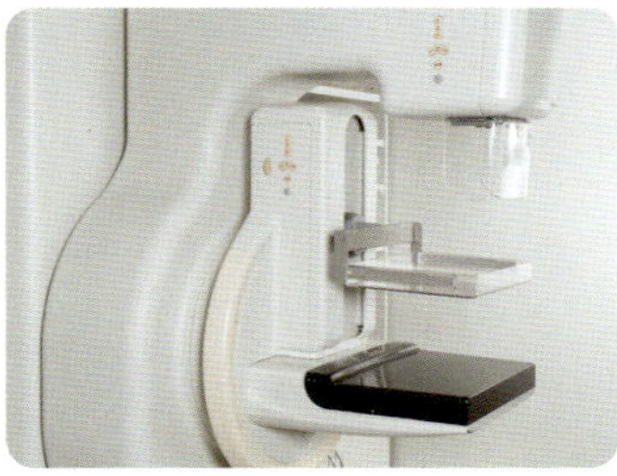

____

3 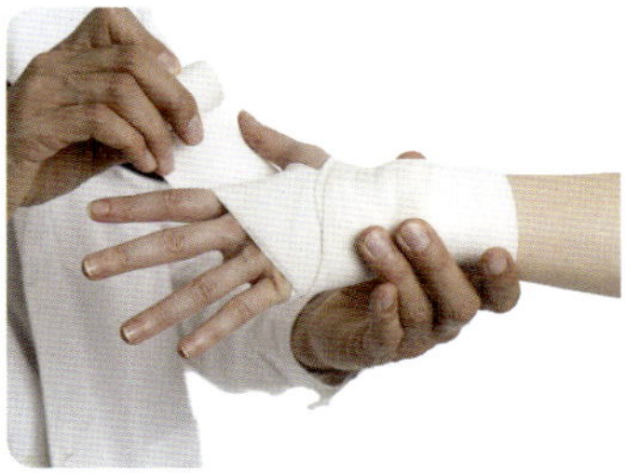

____

Marie Curie

Listen to the talk. Fill in the blanks as you listen.

On November 7, 1867, Maria Sklodowska was born in Poland. Few people have ________________ her. However, lots of people know her by ________________: Marie Curie. Marie Curie was one of ________________ in the early twentieth century.

Marie wanted to become a scientist ________________. But she couldn't do that in her native Poland. So, in 1891, she ________________. She went to a university there. Then, in 1894, she met Pierre Curie. He was a scientist, too. A year later, they got married. They did a number of ________________.

Marie and Pierre did research ________________. They made some new discoveries. In 1903, they ________________ the Nobel Prize in Physics for their work on radiation. Unfortunately, in 1906, Pierre was involved ________________ and died. Marie was ________________ by his death. But she continued her work in science.

In 1911, she received another Nobel Prize. This time, the award was in the ________________. During her research, Marie discovered ________________. They were polonium and radium. Thanks to her two Nobel Prizes, Marie became famous. Many scientists visited her and ________________ with her.

Marie ________________ for the rest of her life. She helped invent a ________________. She also realized that radiation could be helpful in the ________________. When she died in 1934, she was one of the ________________ in the world.

Organizer Listen to the talk again. Then, fill in the blanks with the correct word(s).

Marie Curie

- Was born in ⓐ ____________ and named Maria Sklodowska
- Is ⓑ ____________ by her married name Marie Curie
- Moved to France to study at a university
- Met Pierre Curie and got ⓒ ____________ to him
- Won a Nobel Prize with him for their work on ⓓ ____________
- Received another Nobel Prize in ⓔ ____________
- Discovered two new elements: polonium and radium
- Helped invent ⓕ ____________ X-ray machines

Comprehension

Main Topic

Circle the correct answer.

1 What is the main idea of the talk?

ⓐ Marie Curie won the Nobel Prize twice.

ⓑ Marie Curie and her husband Pierre often worked together.

ⓒ Marie Curie made many scientific accomplishments.

Details

Answer the questions.

2 When did Marie meet Pierre Curie?

ⓐ In 1891

ⓑ In 1894

ⓒ In 1895

3 Which field did Marie Curie NOT win a Nobel Prize in?

ⓐ Biology

ⓑ Physics

ⓒ Chemistry

4 What did Marie Curie help invent?

ⓐ A metal detector

ⓑ A device that detects radiation

ⓒ A portable X-ray machine

5 Fill in the blank with the correct word(s).

Marie and Pierre Curie worked together and won the ________________ in Physics in 1903.

Vocabulary

Match the words and phrases with their definitions.

6 element •	• ⓐ able to be carried
7 portable •	• ⓑ referring to a person's homeland
8 native •	• ⓒ a type of energy that is released in particles or waves
9 radiation •	• ⓓ to be given a prize
10 be awarded •	• ⓔ a substance such as oxygen, carbon, gold, and lead

Listening Skills Practice: Sequencing II

What is sequencing?

Sequencing involves putting the events in a talk in the correct order. Begin with the first event. Then, continue by putting all of the events in the same order that the speaker mentions them. Many speakers use sequencings words. Some common sequencing words are *first*, *next*, *then*, *after that*, and *finally*.

A Listen to the talk again. Then, put the sentences in the correct order.

ⓐ ________ Marie Curie was visited by many scientists.

ⓑ ________ Marie and Pierre Curie won the Nobel Prize in Physics.

ⓒ ________ Marie Curie was awarded the Nobel Prize in Chemistry.

B Listen to an announcement by a news broadcaster related to the topic and answer the questions.

Memo

1 What probably killed Marie Curie?

ⓐ An infection

ⓑ Radiation

ⓒ Cancer

2 In the early 1900s, why did people NOT take safety measures when working with X-rays?

ⓐ They did not know X-rays were dangerous.

ⓑ They thought X-rays could make them stronger.

ⓒ They did not know that X-rays existed.

3 Put the following sentences in the correct order.

ⓐ ________ Marie Curie worked hard to become a great scientist.

ⓑ ________ Marie Curie passed away.

ⓒ ________ Marie Curie won the Nobel Prize in Physics.

Chapter 3

Historical Eras

Unit 09 The Stone Age

Pre-Listening Questions

Answer the following questions.

1 When was the Stone Age?

2 Why do you think it is called the Stone Age?

3 What do you think life in the Stone Age was like?

Vocabulary

Look at the pictures. Write the correct word(s) from the box for each picture.

spear point	ice age	humanoid

1  ______________

2  ______________

3  ______________

The Stone Age

Listen to the talk. Fill in the blanks as you listen.

There have been __________ in history. Now, we live in the Modern Age. It's __________. But today's technology is a fairly __________. For most of human history, people lived primitive lives. In fact, __________ of time in human history is called the Stone Age. During it, humans mostly made __________.

The Stone Age began around __________ ago. Then, modern humans didn't even exist. There were other humanoids alive though. Modern humans __________ later. These humanoids lived in Africa. They made __________ from stone. For instance, they made stone weapons such as __________. They made other tools from stones as well.

Scientists today divide the Stone Age into __________. They are the Paleolithic, Mesolithic, and Neolithic periods. The Paleolithic Period started about three million years ago. It ended around __________. During it, humans were __________. They used very __________.

The Mesolithic Period ended around 10,000 years ago. During it, humans had to survive the last __________. This period ended when humans discovered how to __________. It ended at different times __________.

The Neolithic Period also ended __________. For example, it lasted until 2000 B.C. in some places. This was __________ time in the Stone Age. Humans learned to __________. They started farming as well. So they made permanent settlements. The first human __________ also arose during the Neolithic Period.

Organizer Listen to the talk again. Then, fill in the blanks with the correct word(s).

The Stone Age

- ⓐ __________ Period lasted from 3 million years ago to 40,000 years ago
  - Humans were primitive ⓑ __________
- Mesolithic Period lasted from 40,000 years ago to ⓒ __________ years ago
  - ⓓ __________ when humans learned to grow crops
- Neolithic Period lasted until ⓔ __________ B.C. in some places
  - Humans tamed animals, farmed, and made ⓕ __________ settlements

Comprehension

Main Topic

Circle the correct answer.

1 What is the main idea of the talk?

ⓐ Some experts believe that Stone Age people were more advanced.

ⓑ The Stone Age was a long period of time in which primitive humans lived.

ⓒ The first permanent settlements happened during the Stone Age.

Details

Answer the questions.

2 When did the Stone Age begin?

ⓐ Around three million years ago

ⓑ Around ten million years ago

ⓒ Around thirty million years ago

3 What did NOT happen during the Paleolithic Period?

ⓐ People used simple stone tools.

ⓑ Humans learned how to farm.

ⓒ Humans were hunter-gatherers.

4 Which statement about the Neolithic Period is true?

ⓐ Humans made permanent settlements during it.

ⓑ The last major ice age happened during it.

ⓒ It was the longest period in the Stone Age.

5 Fill in the blank with the correct word(s).

The Stone Age is divided into the Paleolithic, ____________________, and Neolithic periods.

Vocabulary

Match the words and phrases with their definitions.

6 tame	•	• ⓐ a place where a person lives all throughout the year
7 primitive	•	• ⓑ basic; simple
8 hunter-gatherer	•	• ⓒ to teach an animal to live with and to obey humans
9 fairly	•	• ⓓ somewhat; a bit
10 permanent settlement	•	• ⓔ a person who hunts and collects food

Listening Skills Practice: Understanding Organization I

What is understanding organization?

Understanding organization lets a person understand why speakers provide certain information in their talks. Speakers include information for various reasons. For example, they may mention facts to make comparisons, to provide examples, and to make arguments. Listen carefully to understand why speakers mention certain things in their talks.

A **Listen to the talk again. Then, answer the following questions.**

ⓐ Why does the speaker mention spear points?

ⓘ To discuss how Stone Age people made them

ⓘⓘ To give an example of a Stone Age tool

ⓑ Why does the speaker discuss the Neolithic Period?

ⓘ To compare it with the Paleolithic and Mesolithic periods

ⓘⓘ To prove that it lasted for a few thousand years

B **Listen to another talk related to the topic and answer the questions.**

NOTE

1 What is bronze?

ⓐ A combination of gold and silver

ⓑ A combination of copper and tin

ⓒ A combination of platinum and zinc

2 Why does the speaker mention Egypt and Mesopotamia?

ⓐ To state when they entered the Bronze Age

ⓑ To describe the bronze weapons people made in them

ⓒ To explain where both of them are located

3 Why does the speaker mention the Iron Age?

ⓐ To note which culture entered it first

ⓑ To claim it was less advanced than the Bronze Age

ⓒ To say that it came after the Bronze Age

Unit 10 Ancient Greece

Pre-Listening Questions

Answer the following questions.

1 Where is the building in the picture?

2 Why do people remember the ancient Greeks?

3 What do you know about the ancient Greeks?

Vocabulary

Look at the pictures. Write the correct word(s) from the box for each picture.

Socrates	Olympic Games	Alexander the Great

1 

____

2 

____

3 

____

Ancient Greece

Listen to the talk. Fill in the blanks as you listen.

One of the most important ancient civilizations ____________. Greece is located in Southeastern Europe. It lies ____________ of the northern part of the Mediterranean Sea. The ancient Greeks were the ____________ civilization.

Ancient Greek civilization ____________ three separate periods. They are the Archaic, Classical, and Hellenistic periods. The Archaic Period lasted ____________ B.C. to 508 B.C. During it, the poet Homer composed ____________ the *Iliad* and the *Odyssey*. In addition, the ____________ were held during this time.

During the Classical Period, the Greeks began to ____________. The Greeks also established city-states. These were large cities that ____________ around them. The greatest Greek city-state was Athens. It produced many famous ____________, and warriors. Socrates and Plato, the great philosophers, lived during the Classical Period. Athens wasn't the only powerful city-state though. Thebes and Corinth were two others. Sparta was another. Athens and Sparta were ____________. They fought each other in the Peloponnesian War. It was ____________ that lasted from 431 to 404 B.C.

The Hellenistic Period began in ____________ That was the year Alexander the Great died. Alexander and ____________ much of the known world. So Greek culture spread to many places. However, by 146 B.C., the Greeks had weakened while the Romans had ____________. The Romans conquered the Greeks in that year and ____________ to ancient Greece.

Organizer Listen to the talk again. Then, fill in the blanks with the correct word(s).

Ancient Greece

- Archaic Period lasted from 800 to 508 B.C.
  - Homer wrote the *Iliad* and the ⓐ ____________
- ⓑ ____________ Period was when the Greeks started democracy
  - Were ⓒ ____________ such as Athens, Thebes, Corinth, and Sparta
  - Were many great statesmen, scientists, philosophers, and warriors in ⓓ ____________
- Hellenistic Period started in 323 B.C. when Alexander the Great ⓔ ____________
  - Ended in 146 B.C. when the Romans conquered the ⓕ ____________

Comprehension

Main Topic

Circle the correct answer.

1 What is the main topic of the talk?
ⓐ The three main periods in ancient Greece
ⓑ The most famous men in ancient Greece
ⓒ How the ancient Greeks founded Western civilization

Details

Answer the questions.

2 What did NOT happen during the Archaic Period?
ⓐ The Olympic Games started.
ⓑ The Greeks practiced democracy.
ⓒ Homer wrote the *Iliad* and the *Odyssey*.

3 What was the most famous Greek city-state?
ⓐ Sparta
ⓑ Corinth
ⓒ Athens

4 When did the Hellenistic Period begin?
ⓐ When the Peloponnesian War ended
ⓑ When Alexander the Great died
ⓒ When the Romans conquered Greece

5 Fill in the blank with the correct word(s).

The ancient Greeks were the founders of ________________.

Vocabulary

Match the words and phrases with their definitions.

6 epic poem	ⓐ a soldier; a person who is very good at fighting
7 warrior	ⓑ a very long poem
8 statesman	ⓒ to found; to start; to begin
9 establish	ⓓ the land that people in an area know about
10 the known world	ⓔ a politician; a person who excels at representing his or her government

Listening Skills Practice: Understanding Organization II

What is understanding organization?

Understanding organization lets a person understand why speakers provide certain information in their talks. Speakers include information for various reasons. For example, they may mention facts to give explanations, to provide solutions to problems, and to put information into categories. Listen carefully to understand why the speakers mention certain things in their talks.

A Listen to the talk again. Then, answer the following questions.

ⓐ Why does the speaker mention Homer?
- ⓘ To name him as the author of the *Iliad* and the *Odyssey*
- ⓘⓘ To give a short description of his life and works

ⓑ Why does the speaker discuss Athens?
- ⓘ To explain why it was so famous
- ⓘⓘ To talk about its role in creating democracy

B Listen to a tour guide give a talk related to the topic and answer the questions.

Memo

1 What does *molon labe* mean?
- ⓐ Come and take them.
- ⓑ I have not yet begun to fight.
- ⓒ We shall never surrender.

2 Why does the speaker mention King Xerxes?
- ⓐ To say that he was a bad leader
- ⓑ To state that he was the Persian leader
- ⓒ To describe how he became the king

3 Why does the speaker mention the number of Spartans?
- ⓐ To contrast it with the number of Persians
- ⓑ To prove that the Spartans needed more men
- ⓒ To claim that it was impossible for the Spartans to win

Unit
11
The Middle Ages

Pre-Listening Questions

Answer the following questions.

1 What kind of building is in the picture?

2 Who used to live in this kind of building?

3 What do you know about the Middle Ages? What was life in medieval times like?

Vocabulary

Look at the pictures. Write the correct word(s) from the box for each picture.

king	serf	noble

1 

____

2 

____

3 

____

The Middle Ages

Listen to the talk. Fill in the blanks as you listen.

In 476, the Roman Empire fell. It ____________ Germanic barbarians. Yet Rome had been ____________ for many decades before 476. When the Roman Period ended, the ____________. The Middle Ages lasted from around 400 to 1500 in some places.

One major characteristic of the Middle Ages is that ____________. Previously, Rome ____________ much of Europe. But the Middle Ages featured many ____________ instead.

During the Middle Ages, ____________ from Rome was lost. There had been many ____________ in the Roman Empire. But life in medieval times revolved around ____________ and towns. The Church became one of the most ____________. So it dominated most people's lives.

The Middle Ages was ____________. Christian Europeans often had to ____________ invading Muslims. Muslim armies conquered much of Spain. After that, they ____________. But Charles Martel defeated them at the Battle of Tours ____________. Centuries later, the Europeans launched the Crusades. They were a series of wars in the Middle East. The Europeans were ____________ the Muslims out of Jerusalem and the land around it.

In many places, the ____________ was feudalism. ____________ was at the top of this system. Beneath him were his nobles. The king granted the nobles land. They provided him with ____________. Beneath the nobles were serfs. They ____________ for the nobles. The serfs' lives were very difficult.

Organizer Listen to the talk again. Then, fill in the blanks with the correct word(s).

The Middle Ages

- Started after the Roman Period ended
  - Lasted from around 400 to ⓐ ____________
  - Much knowledge from ⓑ ____________ was lost during it
- Was a ⓒ ____________ period
  - Were many wars against invading ⓓ ____________
  - Fought the Crusades in the Middle East
- Had feudalism as a system of government
  - ⓔ ____________ went from kings to nobles to serfs
  - The lives of serfs were very ⓕ ____________

Comprehension

Main Topic

Circle the correct answer.

1 What is the main topic of the talk?

ⓐ The importance of feudalism in the Middle Ages
ⓑ The major historical battles of the Middle Ages
ⓒ Some important features of the Middle Ages

Details

Answer the questions.

2 Where did many people live in the Middle Ages?

ⓐ In very large cities
ⓑ In smaller cities and towns
ⓒ In tiny villages

3 What did Charles Martel do?

ⓐ He defeated some Muslim invaders.
ⓑ He ruled a king of England.
ⓒ He led an army in the Crusades.

4 Which statement about feudalism is NOT true?

ⓐ Nobles voted for who would be king.
ⓑ The king was at the top of the system.
ⓒ Serfs worked the land for nobles.

5 Fill in the blank with the correct word(s).

The Europeans fought the ____________________ to try to get the Muslims out of Jerusalem.

Vocabulary

Match the words and phrases with their definitions.

6 barbarian •	• ⓐ gradually; slowly and constantly
7 dominate •	• ⓑ to be centered on; to focus on
8 conquer •	• ⓒ an uncivilized person
9 revolve around •	• ⓓ to win in battle
10 steadily •	• ⓔ to control; to rule

Listening Skills Practice: Connecting Words I

What are connecting words?

Connecting words combine two or more words, sentences, and phrases. Speakers use connecting words to put similar facts and opinions together. They also make comparisons and contrasts with them. Speakers often use connecting words at the beginnings of sentences. *But*, *so*, *and*, *in addition*, *yet*, and *however* are some common connecting words.

A Use the connecting words in the box to complete the sentences.

so	after that	but

ⓐ Previously, Rome had controlled much of Europe. ________________ the Middle Ages featured many small independent kingdoms instead.

ⓑ The Church became one of the most important parts of society. ________________ it dominated most people's lives.

ⓒ Muslim armies conquered much of Spain. ________________, they invaded France.

B Listen to another talk related to the topic and answer the questions.

NOTE

1 Where did people first start getting sick from the bubonic plague?

ⓐ In Europe
ⓑ In China
ⓒ On the Silk Road

2 Which of the following was a positive result of the Black Death?

ⓐ Around half of all Europeans died.
ⓑ Workers made more money from their labor.
ⓒ It did not happen during the Renaissance.

3 Choose the correct connecting words for the sentences.

ⓐ The bubonic plague was contagious, (so / but) it slowly spread.
ⓑ The Black Death was a terrible time. (But / And) it also had some positive results.
ⓒ The survivors of the Black Death ate better (or / and) became healthier.

Unit 12

The Renaissance

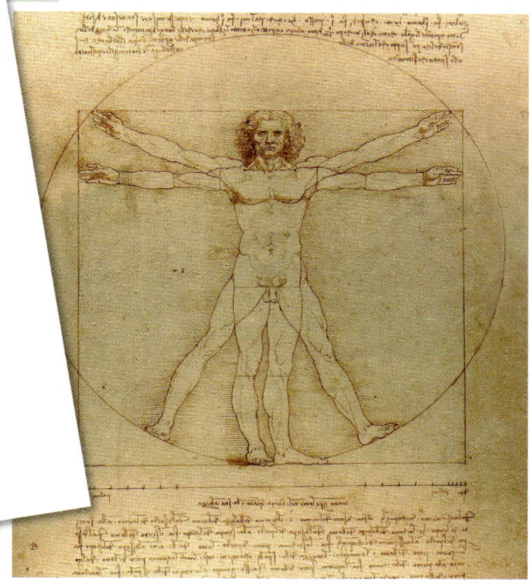

Pre-Listening Questions

Answer the following questions.

1 What can you see in the pictures?

2 Where did the Renaissance start?

3 Do you know any famous people from the Renaissance? What did they do?

Vocabulary

Look at the pictures. Write the correct word(s) from the box for each picture.

text	threaten	scholar

1 

____

2 

____

3 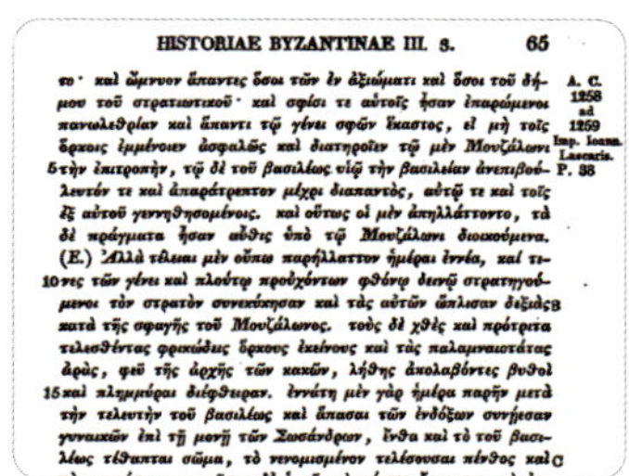

HISTORIAE BYZANTINAE III. 8. 65

το· καὶ ὤμνυον ἅπαντες ὅσοι τῶν ἐν ἀξιώματι καὶ ὅσοι τοῦ δήμου τοῦ στρατιωτικοῦ· καὶ σφίσι τε αὐτοῖς ἦσαν ἐπαρώμενοι πανωλεθρίαν καὶ ἅπαντι τῷ γένει σφῶν ἕκαστος, εἰ μὴ τοῖς ὅρκοις ἐμμένοιεν ἀσφαλῶς καὶ διατηροῖεν τῷ μὲν Μουζάλωνι τὴν ἐπιτροπήν, τῷ δὲ τοῦ βασιλέως υἱῷ τὴν βασιλείαν ἀνεπιβούλευτόν τε καὶ ἀπαράτρεπτον μέχρι διαπαντός, αὐτῷ τε καὶ τοῖς ἐξ αὐτοῦ γεννηθησομένοις. καὶ οὕτως οἱ μὲν ἀπηλλάττοντο, τὰ δὲ πράγματα ἦσαν αὖθις ὑπὸ τῷ Μουζάλωνι διοικούμενα. (E.) Ἀλλὰ τέλειαι μὲν οὔπω παρήλλαττον ἡμέραι ἐννέα, καί τινες τῶν γένει καὶ πλούτῳ προὐχόντων φθόνῳ δεινῷ στρατηγούμενοι τὸν στρατὸν συνεκύκησαν καὶ τὰς αὐτῶν ὥπλισαν δεξιὰς B κατὰ τῆς σφαγῆς τοῦ Μουζάλωνος. τοὺς δὲ χθὲς καὶ πρότριτα τελεσθέντας φρικώδεις ὅρκους ἐκείνους καὶ τὰς παλαμναιοτάτας ἀράς, φεῦ τῆς ἀρχῆς τῶν κακῶν, λήθης ἀπολαβόντες βυθοὶ καὶ πλημμύραι διέφθειραν. ἐννάτη μὲν γὰρ ἡμέρα παρῆν μετὰ τὴν τελευτὴν τοῦ βασιλέως καὶ ἅπασαι τῶν ἐνδόξων συνῆεσαν γυναικῶν ἐπὶ τῇ μονῇ τῶν Σωσάνδρων, ἔνθα καὶ τὸ τοῦ βασιλέως τέθαπται σῶμα, τὸ νενομισμένον τελέσουσαι πένθος καὶ C

A. C. 1258 ad 1259 Imp. Ioann. Lascaris. P. 38

____

The Renaissance

Listen to the talk. Fill in the blanks as you listen.

In the 1300s, the Byzantine Empire was __________. The Ottoman Turks were attacking it __________ and threatening it. As a result, many Byzantines fled the empire. Lots of them moved west and went to Italy. Many of these __________. They brought texts from ancient __________ with them. These texts __________ in the West. The Byzantines reintroduced them. This helped start the Renaissance in Europe around 1400.

The word Renaissance __________." This was a period when there was a __________. Thanks to the texts from ancient times, the Europeans were able to relearn lost knowledge __________. The Renaissance began __________ city-state of Florence. Then, it spread to other places in Italy, such as Rome and Venice. Next, it made its way __________, the Germanic states, England, the Netherlands, and other places.

One __________ of the Renaissance was humanism. It was a new __________. Humanists believed that everyone __________. They also wanted people to learn about the __________, and literature. Humanism __________ how people thought during this period.

There were __________ during the Renaissance. There were improvements in art, science, engineering, and other fields. There were lots of __________ as well. Some of them were so great that they were called __________. A Renaissance Man was someone __________ several fields. Leonardo da Vinci and Michelangelo Buonarroti were two such people.

Organizer Listen to the talk again. Then, fill in the blanks with the correct word(s).

The Renaissance

- Started when Byzantines moved west to Italy and brought old ⓐ __________ with them
- Were texts that had been lost in the West
- Spread throughout ⓑ __________ and then went north to other parts of Europe
- Began in the city-state of Florence, Italy

Features

- Was a new way of thinking called ⓒ __________
- Thought people should be educated in the arts, science, and ⓓ __________
- Were Renaissance Men who excelled in ⓔ __________ fields
- Were improvements in ⓕ __________, science, engineering, and other fields

Comprehension

Main Topic

Circle the correct answer.

1 What is the main idea of the talk?

ⓐ There were many Renaissance Men in Europe.

ⓑ The Renaissance started thanks to the Byzantine Empire.

ⓒ The Renaissance resulted in many changes in Europe.

Details

Answer the questions.

2 Where did the Renaissance begin?

ⓐ In Rome

ⓑ In Venice

ⓒ In Florence

3 What is humanism?

ⓐ The belief that people should be educated in various fields

ⓑ The study of topics that most humans like

ⓒ The idea that humans are the strongest animals on the Earth

4 Which person was NOT a Renaissance Man?

ⓐ Leonardo da Vinci

ⓑ Raphael Sanzio

ⓒ Michelangelo Buonarroti

5 Fill in the blank with the correct word(s).

Many ________________ scholars brought texts from ancient Greece and Rome to Italy.

Vocabulary

Match the words and phrases with their definitions.

6	relearn	•	• ⓐ very intelligent; very smart
7	brilliant	•	• ⓑ to run away
8	excel	•	• ⓒ to be very good at something
9	be in decline	•	• ⓓ to learn something again
10	flee	•	• ⓔ to be getting worse

Listening Skills Practice: Connecting Words II

What are connecting words?

Connecting words combine two or more words, sentences, and phrases. Connecting words let speakers put similar facts or opinions together. They also let speakers make comparisons and contrasts. Many times, speakers use connecting words in the middle of sentences. Some common connecting words are *and*, *but*, *so*, *or*, *when*, and *because*.

A Use the correct connecting words in the box to complete the sentences.

when	such as	and

ⓐ Then, it spread to other places in Italy, ________________ Rome and Venice.

ⓑ This was a period ________________ there was a rebirth in knowledge.

ⓒ Leonardo da Vinci ________________ Michelangelo Buonarroti were two such people.

B Listen to a talk by an art gallery director related to the topic and answer the questions.

Memo

1 What was the topic of most medieval art?

ⓐ Mythology

ⓑ History

ⓒ Religion

2 Which technique did Renaissance artists NOT use?

ⓐ Perspective

ⓑ Proportion

ⓒ Sponging

3 Choose the correct connecting words for the sentences.

ⓐ Renaissance artists made religious works, (but / so) they also painted scenes from mythology.

ⓑ Two of the techniques were perspective (or / and) proportion.

ⓒ The exhibit also some paintings by Caravaggio, Raphael, (and / but) Titian.

Chapter 4

Landmarks

Unit 13 The Eiffel Tower

Listening Skills Practice:
Guessing Unknown Words I

Unit 14 The Leaning Tower of Pisa

Listening Skills Practice:
Guessing Unknown Words II

Unit 15 The Taj Mahal

Listening Skills Practice: Supporting Details I

Unit 16 The Statue of Liberty

Listening Skills Practice: Supporting Details II

Unit 13

The Eiffel Tower

Pre-Listening Questions

Answer the following questions.

1 Where is the Eiffel Tower?

2 When was the Eiffel Tower built?

3 What are some famous landmarks in your country?

Vocabulary

Look at the pictures. Write the correct word(s) from the box for each picture.

elevator	debate	radio tower

1  ______________

2  ______________

3  ______________

The Eiffel Tower

Listen to the talk. Fill in the blanks as you listen.

In 1889, the city of Paris, France, was going to host ____________________. This was considered ____________________. So the organizers wanted to impress people around the world. They decided to erect an imposing building. A contest was held. A design for ____________________ was selected as the winner. Construction began in 1887. ____________________, 1889, the Eiffel Tower was complete.

The Eiffel Tower rose ____________________. When it was finished, it was ____________________ in the world. It remained the highest building until 1930. The Eiffel Tower was built with several thousand ____________________. It had an elevator which took people up to the top. There, they could see nearly sixty kilometers on ____________________.

____________________ the Eiffel Tower was unique, many Parisians in the 1800s hated it. They called it ____________________. Lots of people believed it ruined ____________________.

Originally, the plan was to let the Eiffel Tower ____________________ for twenty years. Then, the tower would ____________________. However, because of its great height, the French started to use it as ____________________. When the twenty-year period came, there was a debate. They decided ____________________ the tower.

Over time, the people of Paris ____________________ about the Eiffel Tower. Today, the Eiffel Tower is ____________________ Paris. It's ____________________ the people of the city. And it's one of the most popular places with tourists in Paris.

Organizer Listen to the talk again. Then, fill in the blanks with the correct word(s).

The Eiffel Tower

- Was built for the ⓐ ____________ World's Fair in Paris
- Is 325 meters high
- Was the world's highest ⓑ ____________ structure
- Was ⓒ ____________ by many Parisians in the 1800s
- Was supposed to stand for ⓓ ____________ years
- Was used as a ⓔ ____________ so didn't get torn down
- Is now a beloved symbol of ⓕ ____________

Comprehension

Main Topic

Circle the correct answer.

1 What is the main topic of the talk?

ⓐ Why people love the Eiffel Tower

ⓑ The history of the Eiffel Tower

ⓒ Who built the Eiffel Tower

Details

Answer the questions.

2 What event was the Eiffel Tower built for?

ⓐ The Olympic Games

ⓑ The World's Fair

ⓒ The Parisian Expo

3 What is NOT true about the Eiffel Tower?

ⓐ It was the highest manmade structure until 1930.

ⓑ It was made of iron.

ⓒ It took ten years to build.

4 How did Parisians feel about the Eiffel Tower in the 1800s?

ⓐ They loved it.

ⓑ They hated it.

ⓒ They thought it was okay.

5 Fill in the blank with the correct word(s).

The Eiffel Tower is beloved by Parisians today and is a __________________ of the city of Paris.

Vocabulary

Match the words and phrases with their definitions.

6 eyesore •	• ⓐ impressive; magnificent
7 manmade structure •	• ⓑ to make an impression on someone
8 ton •	• ⓒ something that looks ugly
9 impress •	• ⓓ a building made by humans
10 imposing •	• ⓔ 2,000 pounds; 1,000 kilograms

Listening Skills Practice: Guessing Unknown Words I

What is guessing unknown words?
Guessing unknown words is a way to learn the meanings of the difficult words in a talk. Listen carefully to the sentences with the difficult words. In addition, pay attention to the sentences that come before and after them. These sentences usually contain clues that can help you figure out the meanings of the words.

A Guess the meaning of the underlined word.

> Today, the Eiffel Tower is a symbol of Paris. It's <u>beloved</u> by the people of the city.

ⓐ adored
ⓑ disliked
ⓒ visited

B Listen to another talk related to the topic and answer the questions.

NOTE

1 What is NOT true about George Washington?
ⓐ People call him "The Father of His Country."
ⓑ He was the first president of the United States.
ⓒ He won every battle in the Revolutionary War.

2 What does the Washington Monument look like?
ⓐ It is an obelisk.
ⓑ It is a pyramid.
ⓒ It is a sphere.

3 Guess the meaning of the underlined word.

> From the top of the Washington Monument, visitors can see the entire city of Washington, D.C. as well as much of the <u>surrounding</u> area.

ⓐ nearby
ⓑ far off
ⓒ scenic

Unit 14

The Leaning Tower of Pisa

Pre-Listening Questions

Answer the following questions.

1 Where is the Leaning Tower of Pisa?

2 Why is it leaning to one side?

3 What else do you know about the Leaning Tower of Pisa?

Vocabulary

Look at the pictures. Write the correct word(s) from the box for each picture.

cathedral	construction	bell

1 

____

2 

____

3 

____

The Leaning Tower of Pisa

Listen to the talk. Fill in the blanks as you listen.

Many of the world's most famous buildings ________________. But there's a tower in Italy that isn't very tall. As ________________, it's only around fifty-six meters tall. This building is renowned ________________: It leans to one side. It's the Leaning Tower of Pisa.

In the Middle Ages, the city of Pisa had a cathedral. The cathedral needed ________________. So in 1173, construction on the bell tower began. Unfortunately, the builders ________________. They didn't realize they were building the tower ________________. As a result, the building ________________ to one side. This happened during the first stage of construction of the tower. That stage ended in 1178. By then, the builders had erected ________________.

Construction on the tower didn't start again ________________. This was the second stage. It ended with ________________ being built. ________________ added two more floors. It ended in 1350. Despite all of the work on the tower, it ________________.

Over the years, there have been ________________ to stop the tower from leaning. They have all failed though. Yet engineers have prevented the tower ________________. Currently, the tower is considered stable and isn't ________________ of falling over.

The fact that the tower leans so much has actually ________________. It's one of ________________ buildings in the world simply because it doesn't ________________.

Organizer Listen to the talk again. Then, fill in the blanks with the correct word(s).

The Leaning Tower of Pisa

- Was intended to be a bell tower for a ⓐ __________
- Construction began in 1173
- Started to lean during the ⓑ __________ stage of construction
- Required ⓒ __________ more stages to be completed

- Have been many attempts to stop the leaning
- All attempts have ⓓ __________
- Isn't in danger of ⓔ __________ though
- Has become ⓕ __________ because it leans

Comprehension

Main Topic

Circle the correct answer.

1 What is the main idea of the talk?

ⓐ There is a good chance that the Leaning Tower of Pisa will fall over soon.

ⓑ Construction on the Leaning Tower of Pisa required three separate stages.

ⓒ The Leaning Tower of Pisa has been leaning almost since it was built.

Details

Answer the questions.

2 What was the purpose of the Leaning Tower of Pisa?

ⓐ To be a bell tower

ⓑ To be a lighthouse

ⓒ To be a cathedral

3 Which statement about the Leaning Tower of Pisa is NOT true?

ⓐ It took more than 100 years to build.

ⓑ It began to lean during the second construction stage.

ⓒ Construction on it began in the Middle Ages.

4 What have engineers prevented the Leaning Tower of Pisa from doing?

ⓐ Falling over

ⓑ Leaning more

ⓒ Sinking into the ground

5 Fill in the blank with the correct word(s).

The Leaning Tower of Pisa leans because the builders were very ________________.

Vocabulary

Match the words and phrases with their definitions.

6	fall over	ⓐ having little or no knowledge of how to do something
7	unsuitable	ⓑ not right for a situation; inappropriate
8	inexperienced	ⓒ to build; to make
9	lean	ⓓ to collapse; to fall down
10	erect	ⓔ to tilt; not to stand up straight but to be slanted

Listening Skills Practice: Guessing Unknown Words II

What is guessing unknown words?

Guessing unknown words is a way to learn the meanings of the difficult words in a talk. Listen carefully to the sentences with the difficult words. In addition, pay attention to the sentences that come before and after them. You can use the information in these sentences to learn the meanings of the difficult words.

A Guess the meaning of the underlined word.

This building is renowned for another reason: It leans to one side.

ⓐ remembered
ⓑ famous
ⓒ constructed

B Listen to a telephone message related to the topic and answer the questions.

Memo

1 What did Eric do today?
ⓐ He went on a tour of Rome.
ⓑ He arrived in Rome on a plane.
ⓒ He played games at the Colosseum.

2 Which statement about the Colosseum is true?
ⓐ It could hold 2,000 people.
ⓑ It had four different levels.
ⓒ The emperor fought gladiators there.

3 Read the sentence. Then, guess the meaning of the underlined word.

It must have been really impressive in the past.

ⓐ large
ⓑ amazing
ⓒ expensive

Unit
15
The Taj Mahal

Pre-Listening Questions

Answer the following questions.

1 Where is the Taj Mahal?

2 Why was the Taj Mahal built?

3 What famous buildings do you know?

Vocabulary

Look at the pictures. Write the correct word(s) from the box for each picture.

precious metals	tomb	builder

1 

____

2 

____

3 

____

The Taj Mahal

Listen to the talk. Fill in the blanks as you listen.

People will do all sorts of things ________________. One man ________________ so much that he had one of the most beautiful buildings on the Earth made ________________. This building is the Taj Mahal.

In 1622, Shah Jahan became the emperor of the Mughal Empire in India. His third wife's name was Mumtaz Mahal. She was ________________. In eighteen years of marriage, she gave birth to ________________. Sadly, when she was ________________, she died while giving birth to her last child. Shah Jahan was devastated ________________. He ordered the Taj Mahal built to ________________ a fitting tomb.

________________ the building together. Then, ________________ from all over the Islamic world. For example, they came from Baghdad, Constantinople, and other places. ________________ men worked on the Taj Mahal. They labored from 1632 to 1653. When they finished, they had truly created "________________." That's what the name Taj Mahal means in English.

The Taj Mahal was made of ________________. Precious metals and gems were used as well. The Taj Mahal even appears to ________________ throughout the day. In fact, in the morning, it looks pink. In the afternoon, it looks white. And in the evening, ________________.

Today, both the emperor and his wife ________________. And millions of people visit the Taj Mahal each year to see the result of ________________ for his wife.

Organizer Listen to the talk again. Then, fill in the blanks with the correct word(s).

The Taj Mahal

- Was built to ⓐ ____________ Mumtaz Mahal
- Was the third wife of Shah Jahan of the Mughal Empire
- Was his ⓑ ____________ wife
- Was built to be her ⓒ ____________

- ⓓ ____________ men labored from 1632 to 1653
- Was made of white marble, ⓔ ____________ metals, and gems
- Appears to change colors ⓕ ____________ the day
- Both Shah Jahan and his wife are buried there

Comprehension

Main Topic

Circle the correct answer.

1 What is the main topic of the talk?

ⓐ The Taj Mahal and why it was made

ⓑ The buildings in the Taj Mahal

ⓒ How the Taj Mahal was designed

Details

Answer the questions.

2 Where did the men who worked on the Taj Mahal come from?

ⓐ Europe

ⓑ Africa

ⓒ The Islamic world

3 What happens to the Taj Mahal during the day?

ⓐ It appears to change colors.

ⓑ It seems to become bigger.

ⓒ It looks like it is getting higher.

4 Who is NOT buried at the Taj Mahal?

ⓐ Shah Jahan

ⓑ Shah Jahan's son

ⓒ Mumtaz Mahal

5 Fill in the blank with the correct word(s).

The Taj Mahal was built because Shah Jahan loved his ________________ very much.

Vocabulary

Match the words and phrases with their definitions.

6	be devastated	ⓐ to work
7	labor	ⓑ appropriate; suitable
8	give birth to	ⓒ to have a child
9	architect	ⓓ to become very sad because of an event
10	fitting	ⓔ a person who designs houses or other buildings

Listening Skills Practice: Supporting Details I

What are supporting details?

Supporting details can provide extra information. Every talk has a main point. Supporting details can help explain the main point of a talk. They can also provide examples and give definitions. Supporting details often follow words like *for example*, *for instance*, *in fact*, and *such as*.

A Fill in the blanks with the words from the box.

for example	as well	in fact

ⓐ The Taj Mahal was made of white marble. Precious metals and gems were used ________________.

ⓑ Builders were imported from all over the Islamic world. ________________, they came from Baghdad, Constantinople, and other places.

ⓒ The Taj Mahal even appears to change colors throughout the day. ________________, in the morning, it looks pink.

B Listen to another talk related to the topic and answer the questions.

NOTE

1 Why are most people interested in the Sydney Opera House?

ⓐ Because of the many events held there

ⓑ Because of its location by the harbor

ⓒ Because of its unique design

2 What did John Utzon do?

ⓐ He designed the Sydney Opera House.

ⓑ He performed in the Sydney Opera House.

ⓒ He paid for the construction of the Sydney Opera House.

3 Match the sentences to complete the supporting details.

ⓐ As a result, there were — ⓘ the Sydney Harbor Bridge.

ⓑ For example, the opera house — ⓘⓘ many delays in its construction.

ⓒ In addition, it's near — ⓘⓘⓘ has many shells made of tile.

Unit 16

The Statue of Liberty

Pre-Listening Questions

Answer the following questions.

1 Where is the Statue of Liberty?

2 What does the Statue of Liberty represent?

3 What are some famous statues that you know about?

Vocabulary

Look at the pictures. Write the correct word(s) from the box for each picture.

tablet	crown	chain

1  ____________

2  ____________

3  ____________

The Statue of Liberty

Listen to the talk. Fill in the blanks as you listen.

One of __________ to recognize in the entire world is in __________. It's on Liberty Island, which is in New York Harbor. __________ is the Statue of Liberty.

On July 4, 1776, the Americans declared their independence __________. They did this __________ the Declaration of Independence. The Americans also __________ of freedom against England. It lasted from 1775 to 1783. During the Revolutionary War, __________ of the Americans.

In 1876, the Americans were __________ of freedom. The French wanted to give a gift to the Americans. French sculptor Frederic Bartholdi was selected to design a statue. He __________ the idea of the Statue of Liberty. He based his design on Libertas. She was the Roman goddess of liberty. She is a __________. She's holding a torch in her right hand. In her left hand, she's __________. On the tablet is the date of the signing of the Declaration of Independence. She's wearing a crown with seven spikes. And there's __________ on the ground at her feet.

The French weren't able to deliver the statue by 1876 though. Instead, the project __________ funding problems. Finally, both the pedestal—the base of the statue—and the statue itself were complete. The statue was dedicated on __________. Since then, it has greeted everyone—both Americans and foreigners—who goes through New York Harbor to enter __________.

Organizer Listen to the talk again. Then, fill in the blanks with the correct word(s).

The Statue of Liberty

- Was made for the United States
  - France had been an ally in America's war of freedom against ⓐ __________
  - Was a ⓑ __________ for when the U.S. was celebrating 100 years of freedom
- Was designed by Frederic Bartholdi
  - Based on the Roman ⓒ __________ Libertas
  - Is a ⓓ __________ of freedom
  - Is a broken chain at her ⓔ __________
  - Is on ⓕ __________ Island in New York Harbor

Comprehension

Main Topic

Circle the correct answer.

1 What is the main idea of the talk?

ⓐ The Statue of Liberty is a symbol of freedom in New York Harbor.

ⓑ The Statue of Liberty was dedicated on October 28, 1886.

ⓒ The Statue of Liberty was designed by Frederic Bartholdi.

Details

Answer the questions.

2 Who did the Americans fight their war of independence against?

ⓐ France

ⓑ Spain

ⓒ England

3 Who was Libertas?

ⓐ The Roman goddess of victory

ⓑ The Roman goddess of freedom

ⓒ The Roman goddess of democracy

4 Which item is the Statue of Liberty NOT holding?

ⓐ A torch

ⓑ A chain

ⓒ A tablet

5 Fill in the blank with the correct word(s).

The Statue of Liberty is located on ________________ in New York Harbor.

Vocabulary

Match the words and phrases with their definitions.

6	ally	ⓐ to be officially opened
7	be dedicated	ⓑ freedom
8	independence	ⓒ a friend
9	pedestal	ⓓ a light that a person carries in his or her hand
10	torch	ⓔ the base of a statue

Listening Skills Practice: Supporting Details II

What are supporting details?
Supporting details can provide extra information. Every talk has a main point. Supporting details can help explain the main point of a talk. They can also provide examples and give definitions. Many times, a talk has several supporting examples.

A Write MI (main idea) or SD (supporting detail).

ⓐ ________ The Statue of Liberty is wearing a crown.
ⓑ ________ The Statue of Liberty is a symbol of freedom.
ⓒ ________ There is a broken chain at the feet of the Statue of Liberty.

B Listen to a talk by a guest speaker related to the topic and answer the questions.

NOTE

1 Where did Walter Schnell and his family come from?
ⓐ The United States
ⓑ Germany
ⓒ Russia

2 Where did immigrants to the United States go first?
ⓐ To the Statue of Liberty
ⓑ To New York City
ⓒ To Ellis Island

3 Fill in the blanks to complete the supporting details.
ⓐ Walter Schnell and his family took a ship across the ________________.
ⓑ They had to visit ________________ first.
ⓒ Before they went there, they saw the ________________.

Chapter 5

The Ocean

Unit 17 Coral Reefs

Pre-Listening Questions

Answer the following questions.

1 What can you see in the picture?

2 Where are coral reefs located?

3 Why do many animals live in coral reefs?

Vocabulary

Look at the pictures. Write the correct word(s) from the box for each picture.

sea creature	shelter	marine biologist

1 

____

2 

____

3 

____

Coral Reefs

Listen to the talk. Fill in the blanks as you listen.

Coral reefs are some of the most vital ecosystems on the planet. They exist in ____________________ of places though. The reason is that they can only survive ____________________. Coral reefs thrive in water that's between sixteen and thirty degrees Celsius. And they also exist only ____________________. As a result, only ____________________ of the bottom of the ocean is covered with coral.

Still, despite covering a tiny area, coral reefs provide ____________________ for thousands of aquatic species. In fact, marine biologists estimate that ____________________ of all ocean animals live in or ____________________.

Most coral reefs are fairly ____________________. Yet some can be vast. For instance, the Great Barrier Reef ____________________ is enormous. It's a system that contains more than ____________________. It's about 2,500 kilometers long.

Coral reefs are ____________________ for several reasons. First, the hard corals provide ____________________ for small fish. These let the fish evade predators. In fact, most large predators cannot even swim in coral reefs since the hard ____________________ them. Many fish—and other animals—also lay their eggs in coral reefs. When the eggs hatch, the fish can grow up in relative safety. Finally, coral reefs are rich in nutrients. So the animals living in them have ____________________ of food. These features make coral reefs ____________________ to live for many sea creatures.

Organizer Listen to the talk again. Then, fill in the blanks with the correct word(s).

Coral Reefs

- Are vital ⓐ ____________
- Live in warm water between 16 and ⓑ ____________ degrees Celsius
- ⓒ ____________ live in shallow water
- A small percentage of the Earth's oceans has coral reefs

- Around 25% of all ocean animals live in or around them
- Provide hiding places for ⓓ ____________ fish due to hard corals
- Fish and other animals lay their ⓔ ____________ in them
- Are many nutrients, so animals have a constant ⓕ ____________ supply

Comprehension

Main Topic

Circle the correct answer.

1 What is the main idea of the talk?

ⓐ Coral reefs are important ecosystems since many animals live in them.

ⓑ The largest coral reef in the world is the Great Barrier Reef in Australia.

ⓒ There are many different species of fish living in coral reefs.

Details

Answer the questions.

2 Which statement about coral reefs is NOT true?

ⓐ They only exist in shallow water.

ⓑ They need warm water to grow well.

ⓒ They can survive in fresh water.

3 About what percentage of all ocean animals live in or around coral reefs?

ⓐ Five percent

ⓑ Twenty-five percent

ⓒ Forty percent

4 How do coral reefs protect animals from predators?

ⓐ The sharp corals cut the predators.

ⓑ Predators cannot swim in very shallow water.

ⓒ The water in the reefs is too warm for predators.

5 Fill in the blank with the correct word(s).

A large number of ________________ live in and around the planet's coral reefs.

Vocabulary

Match the words and phrases with their definitions.

6	evade	ⓐ an animal that lives in the water
7	rich	ⓑ to do well
8	aquatic species	ⓒ having a lot of; wealthy
9	thrive	ⓓ to avoid; to keep away from someone or something
10	vital	ⓔ very important

Listening Skills Practice: Dictation I

What is dictation?

Dictation is writing down the exact words that a person says. Sometimes you need to know every word in a sentence. Use dictation to write them down. Dictation can help you improve your listening skills. It can also make your spelling and punctuation much better.

A Listen to the talk again. Practice dictation by writing the exact words the speaker says.

Coral reefs are some of the most vital ecosystems on the planet. They exist in a limited number of places though. The reason is that ⓐ ______________________________ ______. Coral reefs thrive in water that's ⓑ ______________________________ ______. And they also exist only in shallow water. As a result, ⓒ ________________ ________________ is covered with coral.

B Listen to a talk related to the topic and answer the questions.

NOTE

1 Where is Hanauma Bay?

ⓐ In Hawaii

ⓑ In Cuba

ⓒ In Guam

2 What can visitors to Hanauma Bay NOT do?

ⓐ Go swimming

ⓑ Go snorkeling

ⓒ Go boating

3 Listen to the talk again. Practice dictation by writing the exact words the speaker says.

ⓐ One of the most popular places ______________________________.

ⓑ These include ______________________________.

ⓒ By banning those activities, ______________________________.

Unit 18

The Mariana Trench

Pre-Listening Questions

Answer the following questions.

1 How deep do you think the submersible in the picture is?

2 Where is the Mariana Trench?

3 What do you think the bottom of the ocean is like?

Vocabulary

Look at the pictures. Write the correct word(s) from the box for each picture.

survey	submersible	tin can

1 

____

2 

____

3 

____

The Mariana Trench

Listen to the talk. Fill in the blanks as you listen.

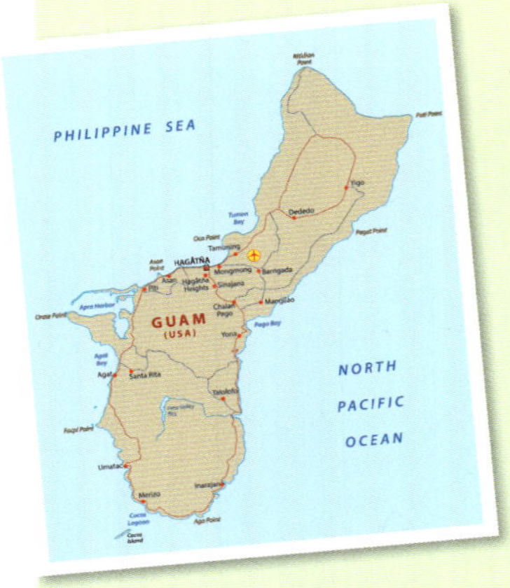

Guam is an island in ____________ of the Pacific Ocean. It lies ____________ and east of the Philippines. Around 330 kilometers southwest of Guam is the Mariana Trench. This is ____________ in the world's oceans. It descends at least ____________ sea level.

The Mariana Trench was first surveyed in 1951. ____________ named the *Challenger II* discovered the deepest part of the trench. The crew named the area Challenger Deep. Since that time, many other ships ____________ the area. They learned that it's ____________ long. It also has an average width of nearly seventy kilometers.

Because the trench is so deep, humans couldn't ____________ of it for many years. The reason concerns ____________. Thousands of meters beneath the surface, the water pressure is so great that ____________ survive. In fact, the water pressure would crush a submarine like it's ____________. However, in recent years, ____________ submersibles have been able to reach the bottom of the Mariana Trench.

These vehicles brought back valuable—and surprising—information. For instance, there are many hot-water vents in the trench. Most of the water there is ____________. Yet the vents provide pockets of ____________. That lets ____________ called microbes live there. There are even ____________ there. Scientists had previously thought that ____________ that deep. But there's an abundance of life in the Mariana Trench.

Organizer Listen to the talk again. Then, fill in the blanks with the correct word(s).

The Mariana Trench

- Is located in the ⓐ ____________ Ocean
- Is south of Japan and ⓑ ____________ of the Philippines
- Descends 10,900 meters ⓒ ____________ sea level

- Was surveyed in 1951 by the *Challenger II*
- Discovered the Challenger Deep: the ⓓ ____________ part of the trench

- Humans could not ⓔ ____________ it for a long time
- ⓕ ____________ is too great in the trench
- Submersibles have reached the bottom lately

Comprehension

Main Topic

Circle the correct answer.

1 What is the main topic of the talk?

ⓐ The Mariana Trench and its characteristics

ⓑ How the Mariana Trench was discovered

ⓒ Where the Mariana Trench is located

Details

Answer the questions.

2 What did the *Challenger II* do?

ⓐ It surveyed 2,500 kilometers of the Mariana Trench.

ⓑ It sent a submersible to the bottom of Challenger Deep.

ⓒ It found the deepest part of the Mariana Trench.

3 Why could humans NOT explore the bottom of the Mariana Trench for so long?

ⓐ Because of the water pressure

ⓑ Because of the lack of oxygen

ⓒ Because of the darkness

4 Where do many animals in the Mariana Trench live?

ⓐ In small caves

ⓑ Near hot-water vents

ⓒ By underwater volcanoes

5 Fill in the blank with the correct word(s).

The Mariana Trench is located in the Pacific Ocean near the island of ________________.

Vocabulary

Match the words and phrases with their definitions.

6 trench	ⓐ a tiny creature that can be seen only with a microscope
7 microbe	ⓑ a deep ditch or hole
8 descend	ⓒ a large number of living creatures
9 valuable	ⓓ to go down
10 an abundance of life	ⓔ worth a lot

Listening Skills Practice: Dictation II

What is dictation?

Dictation is writing down the exact words that a person says. Sometimes you need to know every word in a sentence. The reason is that all of the information is important. Use dictation to write down all of the words. Dictation can improve your listening skills as well as your grammar.

A Listen to the talk again. Practice dictation by writing the exact words the speaker says.

The Mariana Trench was first surveyed in 1951. A British ship named the *Challenger II* ⓐ ____________________. The crew named the area Challenger Deep. Since that time, ⓑ ____________________. They learned that it's more than 2,500 kilometers long. It also has ⓒ ____________________.

B Listen to a talk from a newscaster related to the topic and answer the questions.

Memo

1 What do most people know James Cameron for?
ⓐ Acting in movies
ⓑ Directing movies
ⓒ Exploring the ocean

2 What did James Cameron do for the first time?
ⓐ He went to the bottom of the Mariana Trench by himself.
ⓑ He swam to the bottom of the Mariana Trench.
ⓒ He took a crew of several people to the bottom of the Mariana Trench.

3 Listen to the talk again. Practice dictation by writing the exact words the speaker says.
ⓐ They made more money ____________________.
ⓑ He went to the bottom of the ocean ____________________.
ⓒ For instance, he discovered ____________________.

Unit 19

Deep-Sea Creatures

Pre-Listening Questions

Answer the following questions.

1 Where do you think the animals in the pictures live?

2 What is unique about these animals?

3 What kinds of animals live deep beneath the sea?

Vocabulary

Look at the pictures. Write the correct word(s) from the box for each picture.

coelacanth	shallow	anglerfish

1 

____

2 

____

3 

____

Deep-Sea Creatures

Listen to the talk. Fill in the blanks as you listen.

Near shore, the oceans are shallow. However, a few kilometers off shore, they ____________________. In many places, the oceans are several kilometers deep. ____________________ can reach that deep beneath the surface. In addition, the conditions are harsh. The water ____________________. The water pressure is intense. And there are ____________________ for fish. Nevertheless, many animals live deep ____________________ of the ocean. We call them deep-sea creatures.

There are ____________________ of bacteria that live ____________________. But fish live there, too. There are several types of fish. Two are ____________________ and fish that use bioluminescence.

Living fossils are fish that have been on the Earth for millions of years yet ____________________. The coelacanth is a living fossil. It was alive more than ____________________ ago when the dinosaurs were alive. In fact, scientists have found coelacanth fossils 350 million years old. The coelacanth ____________________ during that time. The frilled shark is another living fossil. It lives more than ____________________ beneath the surface. It resembles the frilled sharks that lived millions of years ago.

Other deep-sea creature use bioluminescence. This means they can create ____________________. Deep underwater, ____________________. So these animals evolved to be able to make their own light. The anglerfish can create light. It ____________________ to attract other fish. Then, it catches and ____________________. The lanternfish and giant flashlight fish can both make light, too.

Organizer **Listen to the talk again. Then, fill in the blanks with the correct word(s).**

Living Fossils

- Have been on the Earth for ⓐ____________ of years but have not evolved much
- Frilled shark resembles sharks from millions of years ago
- Coelacanth was alive 65 million years ago along with ⓑ____________
  - Has changed ⓒ____________ in 350 million years

Bioluminescence

- Can create own light
- Evolved to make light since sea is so ⓓ____________
- Lanternfish and ⓔ____________ can make own light
- Anglerfish creates light to ⓕ____________ fish to eat

Comprehension

Main Topic

Circle the correct answer.

1 What is the main idea of the talk?

ⓐ Some fish are able to use their bodies to make light.

ⓑ The coelacanth is considered a living fossil.

ⓒ A wide variety of fish live deep under the sea.

Details

Answer the questions.

2 What kind of animal is the frilled shark?

ⓐ A living fossil

ⓑ An extinct animal

ⓒ A dinosaur

3 What is NOT true about animals that use bioluminescence?

ⓐ They can create their own light.

ⓑ They may use their light to hunt animals.

ⓒ They have very poor eyesight.

4 Which of the following animals uses bioluminescence?

ⓐ The coelacanth

ⓑ The anglerfish

ⓒ The frilled shark

5 Fill in the blank with the correct word(s).

Lots of bacteria as well as several types of ________________ live deep underwater.

Vocabulary

Match the words and phrases with their definitions.

6 water pressure •	• ⓐ very; extremely
7 incredibly •	• ⓑ the ability of an organism to create its own light
8 bioluminescence •	• ⓒ the power that water has over the area it is in
9 barely •	• ⓓ severe; cruel
10 harsh •	• ⓔ hardly; scarcely

Listening Skills Practice: Classification I

What is classification?

Classification lets you put people, places, and things into groups. Many talks include information about two or more groups. These groups have their own characteristics. Listen carefully to the talk. Then, write the correct characteristics for each group.

A Listen to the talk again. Then, complete the classification charts.

Living Fossils

- One is the coelacanth
- Was alive 65 ⓐ ____________ years ago
- Has ⓑ ____________ little in 350 million years
- One is the frilled shark
- ⓒ ____________ frilled sharks from millions of years ago

Bioluminescence

- Happens when an animal creates its own ⓓ ____________
- Is ⓔ ____________ deep under the sea, so animals need light
- ⓕ ____________ makes light to hunt other fish
- Lanternfish and giant flashlight fish also use bioluminescence

B Listen to another talk related to the topic and answer the questions.

NOTE

1 According to the teacher, where do some animals live?

ⓐ In the hottest deserts

ⓑ On the highest mountains

ⓒ Inside volcanoes

2 How big are microbes?

ⓐ Very large

ⓑ Average size

ⓒ Very small

3 Complete the classification chart about microbes.

Microbes

- Are extremely ⓐ ____________
- Include ⓑ ____________, fungi, and viruses
- Live in the ⓒ ____________
- Some are ⓓ ____________ to humans
- ⓔ ____________ are trying to learn how they can survive so high in the air

Unit 20

Sharks

Pre-Listening Questions

Answer the following questions.

1 What kind of shark is in the picture?

2 What are some other species of sharks?

3 What else do you know about sharks?

Vocabulary

Look at the pictures. Write the correct word(s) from the box for each picture.

shark attack	tiger shark	scuba diving

1  ______________

2  ______________

3  ______________

Sharks

Listen to the talk. Fill in the blanks as you listen.

In 1975, the movie *Jaws* came out. It told the story of a __________ that was attacking people. After watching the movie, millions of people were afraid to __________. They shouldn't have been. Worldwide, there are only about __________ per year. And __________ people die from shark attacks each year.

There are hundreds of species of sharks. Most of them __________. Yet there are a few sharks that do attack humans. The __________ of them are great white sharks, tiger sharks, and bull sharks. __________ nearly all shark attacks on humans.

Great white sharks are __________ creatures in the ocean. They can __________ eight meters long and weigh more than three tons. They have __________ and attack their prey __________. They often swim near the shore. Great whites account for around half of all shark attacks each year.

Tiger sharks are smaller than great whites. They grow to be __________ in length. They live __________. They're dangerous to people who __________ and swimming in places such as Hawaii.

Bull sharks are slightly more than two meters long. But they're very dangerous. They often swim __________. They even swim __________ sometimes. They can swim in water less than one meter deep. They're also __________, so they sometimes attack people who are close to shore.

Organizer Listen to the talk again. Then, fill in the blanks with the correct word(s).

Shark Attacks

- Are about ⓐ __________ per year
  - ⓑ __________ about 20 people per year
- Most sharks are ⓒ __________ man-eaters
  - Are three main species that attack humans
    - Great white sharks can be 8 meters long and weigh ⓓ __________
    - Bull sharks swim close to shore and are ⓕ __________
    - Tiger sharks live in ⓔ __________ waters

Comprehension

Main Topic

Circle the correct answer.

1 What is the main topic of the talk?

ⓐ How to avoid being attacked by a shark

ⓑ The sharks that most commonly attack humans

ⓒ Why some sharks often attack humans

Details

Answer the questions.

2 About how many shark attacks are there around the world each year?

ⓐ 20

ⓑ 50

ⓒ 100

3 Which of the following sharks is NOT a man-eating shark?

ⓐ The bull shark

ⓑ The nurse shark

ⓒ The tiger shark

4 What is true about the great white shark?

ⓐ It is the largest shark in the world.

ⓑ It has more than 3,000 teeth.

ⓒ It attacks fewer humans than tiger sharks.

5 Fill in the blank with the correct word(s).

There are hundreds of species of sharks, but few of them are ________________.

Vocabulary

Match the words and phrases with their definitions.

6	aggressive	ⓐ a shark that attacks and kills humans
7	fearsome creature	ⓑ violent
8	be responsible for	ⓒ each; every
9	man-eating shark	ⓓ to be the cause of
10	per	ⓔ an animal that scares other animals

Listening Skills Practice: Classification II

What is classification?

Classification lets you put information about people, places, and things into different categories. People, places, and things often have different features. Listen carefully to the talk. Then, put each feature into the correct classification. Classification can help you understand more about the people, places, and things.

A Listen to the talk again. Then, complete the classification charts.

Great White Shark
- Can be 8 meters long and weigh 3 tons
- Has ⓐ ____________ teeth
- Swims near shore
- Is responsible for ⓑ ____________ of all shark attacks

Tiger Shark
- Is ⓒ ____________ long
- Lives in ⓓ ____________ waters
- May attack people scuba diving and swimming

Bull Shark
- Is 2 meters long
- Is very ⓔ ____________
- Swims close to shore and in fresh water
- Is very ⓕ ____________

B Listen to a news report related to the topic and answer the questions.

Memo

1 What happened to the woman?

ⓐ A man hit her in the nose.

ⓑ A shark attacked her.

ⓒ She was fishing near shore.

2 What did the man do?

ⓐ He hit the shark in the nose.

ⓑ He called for help.

ⓒ He pulled the woman out of the water.

3 Complete the classification charts about what to do if a shark attacks.

What to Do If a Shark Attacks
- Hit the shark in its ⓐ ____________, gills, or nose
- Stay ⓑ ____________
- Don't wave your ⓒ ____________ around
- Don't try to ⓓ ____________ faster than the shark
- Get out of the ⓔ ____________ quickly

Answers

Answers

Chapter 1 Amazing Places

Unit 01 The Amazon Rainforest

p. 11

Pre-Listening Questions Sample Answer

1 It's in South America. I think it's in Brazil and some other countries.
2 Lots of animals live there. I know there are many snakes, lizards, birds, and insects. There are also many kinds of mammals.
3 It has lots of trees. And some people are cutting down parts of the rainforest.

Vocabulary

1 native Indian
2 jungle floor
3 canopy

p. 12

Script

M Teacher: The Amazon River starts in the Andes Mountains in South America and flows to the Atlantic Ocean. It's the second largest river in the world. There are also more than 1,000 rivers that connect to it. The Amazon Rainforest surrounds much of the Amazon River. It's the world's largest rainforest. Most of it is in Brazil. But parts of it are in eight other countries in South America.

The Amazon Rainforest is filled with tall trees that form a thick canopy. Some of these trees rise to heights of around seventy meters. The jungle floor is also covered with all kinds of vegetation. Scientists believe that 40,000 plant species live in the rainforest.

A diverse amount of wildlife lives in the Amazon Rainforest. About ten percent of all of the animal species on the planet live in the rainforest. This includes around twenty percent of all bird species. More than 2.5 million insect species live there. Numerous kinds of reptiles, fish, and mammals live there, too. I think it's impressive how so many animals live in one place.

Some humans even live in the Amazon Rainforest. In fact, there are many tribes of native Indians living in the jungle there. Some of these tribes have never made contact with any other humans. That's unbelievable. These people live very primitive lives. They hunt and fish for meat. And they gather fruits, nuts, and berries from the jungle. They don't know anything about modern life.

Organizer

ⓐ Surrounds ⓑ South
ⓒ thick ⓓ plants
ⓔ insect ⓕ primitive

p. 13

Comprehension

1 ⓐ 2 ⓐ 3 ⓒ
4 ⓑ 5 Andes Mountains
6 ⓓ 7 ⓐ 8 ⓔ
9 ⓑ 10 ⓒ

p. 14

Listening Skills Practice: Fact and Opinion I

A ⓐ F ⓑ O ⓒ O

B

Script

W Teacher: There are many great waterfalls around the world. Niagara Falls in North America is amazing to see. Victoria Falls in Africa is enormous. I loved visiting both waterfalls. But I believe the most remarkable waterfall in the world is Angel Falls. It's located deep in the jungle in Venezuela in South America. Angel Falls is the world's highest waterfall. There's a drop of 979 meters at the falls. That's nearly one kilometer. It's also nineteen times higher than Niagara Falls. Every year, large numbers of tourists visit Angel Falls. Many of them hike through the jungle to see it. Others fly there and view the falls from an airplane. It's a breathtaking sight when you see it for the first time. I've been there three times, and I had a great time on each of my visits. I can't wait to go back in the future.

1 ⓒ
2 ⓑ
3 ⓐ ⓘⓘⓘ ⓑ ⓘⓘ ⓒ ⓘ

Unit 02 The Grand Canyon

p. 15

Pre-Listening Questions Sample Answer

1 It's in Arizona. That's a state in the U.S.
2 I think it formed because of a river. But I'm not really sure.
3 It's millions of years old.

Vocabulary

1 rafting
2 canyon
3 hike

p. 16

Script

W Teacher: *The Colorado River runs through the southwestern part of the United States. Millions of years ago, the land it flowed through was flat. Then, the river slowly began eroding the land. Over time, it washed away large amounts of land. A canyon then formed. Today, we know it as the Grand Canyon. It's one of the seven natural wonders of the world. And it's a place I believe everyone should visit at least once. You will love the Grand Canyon if you go there.*

The Grand Canyon is located in the American state of Arizona. It's nearly 500 kilometers long. It's more than 1,800 meters deep in many places. And it's around twenty-nine kilometers wide in some places. At the bottom of the canyon, the Colorado River still flows through it on its way to the Gulf of California.

In the past, many Native American tribes lived in the Grand Canyon. Today, only a few Native Americans live there. But the entire Grand Canyon is now a national park. So it's a protected area. More than five million visitors from around the world visit the Grand Canyon each year. Most of them stay on the southern rim. The northern rim gets fewer visitors. I think the northern rim has better views than the southern rim though. The majority of tourists stay at the top of the Grand Canyon. A few hike all the way to the bottom. And some even go rafting through the Grand Canyon.

Organizer

ⓐ Formed ⓑ erosion
ⓒ wide ⓓ national
ⓔ visitors ⓕ hike

p. 17

Comprehension

1 ⓐ 2 ⓐ 3 ⓑ
4 ⓒ 5 millions

6 ⓔ 7 ⓓ 8 ⓐ
9 ⓒ 10 ⓑ

p. 18

Listening Skills Practice: Fact and Opinion II

A ⓐ O ⓑ F ⓒ O

B

Script

M Tour Guide: *Good morning, everyone. I hope you're ready because you're going to have the time of your life today. We're going to go rafting down the Colorado River. And we're going to go through some parts of the Grand Canyon. You're going to get a view of the Grand Canyon that few people ever experience: You're going to see it from the very bottom. Now, let me tell you about the tour. We're going to be rafting in calm water. So there won't be any rapids. You don't need to worry about that. We're going to stop a couple of times to look at some ancient Indian ruins in the canyon. Be sure to take pictures. The ruins are fascinating. We're going to have lunch at the bottom of the canyon, too. Okay. That's enough talking. Let's get started. Everyone get in the raft, please.*

1 ⓑ
2 ⓒ
3 ⓐ ⓘⓘ ⓑ ⓘⓘⓘ ⓒ ⓘ

Unit 03 The Serengeti

p. 19

Pre-Listening Questions Sample Answer

1 It's somewhere in Africa. I don't know the country it's in though.
2 I can see lions in the first picture. In the second picture, there are some birds and really big mammals. I don't know their names though.

3 I think it must be dangerous because there are so many large animals there.

Vocabulary

1 plain
2 hyena
3 wildebeest

p. 20

Script

W Teacher: Africa is the world's second largest continent. It has an interesting geography. For instance, there are desert lands in the north. In the central region, there are rainforests. And in the eastern part of the continent, there is a vast plain. This area is so large that people call it Siringitu. That means "endless plain." The English word Serengeti comes from it.

The Serengeti is located in Tanzania and Kenya. It covers an area of around 30,000 square kilometers. Most of the Serengeti is flat grassland. There are some wooded areas, wetlands, and hilly areas. Yet the land is mostly flat with few trees for as far as the eye can see.

The Serengeti is teeming with wildlife. In fact, some of the largest land animals on the planet live there. Large numbers of elephants, hippopotamuses, giraffes, and rhinoceroses live there. Yet their numbers are small in comparison with the huge herds of other animals that live in the Serengeti. There are herds of zebras, wildebeests, gazelles, and buffalos that contain hundreds of thousands of animals.

There are also large numbers of predators in the Serengeti. Great cats such as lions, leopards, and cheetahs prowl the land. Hyenas and jackals live there in large numbers. The rivers and lakes are filled with vicious crocodiles. There are all kinds of smaller predators as well. They spend much of their time hunting the prey animals that live in the Serengeti.

Organizer

ⓐ Africa ⓑ Kenya
ⓒ giraffes ⓓ predators
ⓔ lions ⓕ crocodiles

p. 21

Comprehension

1 ⓑ 2 ⓒ 3 ⓑ
4 ⓐ 5 predators
6 ⓒ 7 ⓔ 8 ⓐ
9 ⓑ 10 ⓓ

p. 22

Listening Skills Practice: Paraphrasing I

A ⓐ

B

Script

W Teacher: Every year, the Great Migration takes place in the Serengeti. Animals migrate to new lands. They do that to find grass and other vegetation to feed on. The animals migrate because of the rain patterns in the Serengeti. The Great Migration involves more than two million large herbivores. There are more than one million wildebeests. Large herds of zebras, gazelles, and other animals migrate as well. The Great Migration covers a large part of the Serengeti. It's a dangerous time for many animals. Large groups of predators, such as lions, follow the herd. The animals also have to cross rivers full of crocodiles. Many animals don't survive the trip. But others do. The Great Migration takes the animals in a big circle. They end up right where they started. And they do the same trip the next year.

1 ⓑ
2 ⓐ
3 ⓑ

Unit 04 The Dead Sea

p. 23

Pre-Listening Questions Sample Answer

1 It's in the Middle East. I think it's in Israel.
2 The woman is floating in the water and reading a book.
3 I know that the water in it is really salty.

Vocabulary

1 plateau
2 surface
3 float

p. 24

Script

M Teacher: *One of the most unique places in the world is found on the border between Israel and Jordan in the Middle East. It's the Dead Sea. The Dead Sea lies between plateaus east and west of it. The Jordan River flows into it from the north. And some small streams flow into it in from the east. The Dead Sea is around eighty kilometers long and eighteen kilometers wide at some points.*

The Dead Sea isn't actually a sea. It's a very large lake. But it has a number of characteristics that make it notable. First, it's the lowest place on the Earth. The surface of the Dead Sea is more than 400 meters below sea level. In addition, no fish or plants live in the Dead Sea. Sometimes fish swim into the Dead Sea from the Jordan River or various streams. They die almost instantly.

The reason is that the Dead Sea has a very high salt content. Water flows into the Dead Sea. But no water flows out. Over time, some of the water evaporates. But the salt and various minerals remain. The salt content in some parts of the Dead Sea is about thirty-five percent. This means that thirty-five percent of the water is really salt. It's so salty that people can easily float on the water of the Dead Sea. Many people even visit the Dead Sea because of the salt water. They claim it can heal all sorts of physical problems.

Organizer

ⓐ border ⓑ streams
ⓒ 18 ⓓ lake
ⓔ lowest ⓕ salty

p. 25

Comprehension

1 ⓐ 2 ⓑ 3 ⓐ
4 ⓒ 5 physical problems

6 ⓓ 7 ⓑ 8 ⓔ
9 ⓐ 10 ⓒ

p. 26

Listening Skills Practice: Paraphrasing II

A ⓒ

B

Script

W Tour Guide: *Today, we're going to sail around some of the reefs near Belize. We're also going to visit the Great Blue Hole. I'm sure you'll all be amazed by it. The Great Blue Hole is more than 300 meters in diameter. It forms a nearly perfect circle. But that's not the best part. It's an underwater sinkhole, so it goes down to a depth of more than 120 meters. It's considered one of the greatest places in the world for scuba diving. We're not going to do any scuba diving today though. But we are going to sail right on top of the Great Blue Hole. So you'll get a chance to see it from up close. But before we go there, we're going to do some snorkeling in a nearby reef. So let's set sail in order to get to that reef within the next half hour.*

1 ⓒ
2 ⓒ
3 ⓑ

Chapter 2 Great Scientists

Unit 05 Hippocrates

p. 29

Pre-Listening Questions Sample Answer

1 The doctor is talking to a patient.
2 He was a doctor in ancient Greece.
3 I think he made the Hippocratic Oath a long time ago. Doctors today still say it.

Vocabulary

1 observation
2 sickness
3 graduate

p. 30

Script

W Teacher: *Thousands of years ago, no one knew why people got sick. People often blamed their illnesses on various gods and goddesses. They believed that deities got upset and made people sick. In addition, many people died from minor illnesses. Around thirty percent of all babies died before they were a year old. And most people only lived until they were in their forties.*

Yet one man didn't believe the myths about how people got sick. Instead, he based his ideas on medicine by observing sick people. This man was Hippocrates. He was a Greek from the island of Cos. He was born around 460 B.C. And he passed away around 377 B.C.

During Hippocrates's long life, he had a tremendous affect on the study of medicine. In fact, people call him "the father of modern medicine." He transformed the study of medicine from a field based on superstition to one based on observation. He thought that sicknesses and diseases had natural causes. So he tried to figure them out. Hippocrates learned how to treat several diseases. And he made sure to write down everything that he learned. In that way, he shared his knowledge with others. Thanks to him, the Greeks learned a great deal about medical science.

Even today, doctors remember Hippocrates. When most doctors graduate from medical school, they take the Hippocratic Oath. They promise to do no harm to their patients and to help them to the best of their ability.

Organizer

ⓐ gods
ⓑ babies
ⓒ 460
ⓓ father
ⓔ harm
ⓕ diseases

p. 31

Comprehension

1 ⓒ
2 ⓑ
3 ⓐ
4 ⓒ
5 Hippocratic Oath

6 ⓐ
7 ⓔ
8 ⓓ
9 ⓑ
10 ⓒ

p. 32

Listening Skills Practice: Details I

A ⓐ illnesses, babies
ⓑ Hippocrates, medicine
ⓒ diseases, wrote

B

Script

M Teacher: Like the Greeks, the Romans cared a lot about learning. The greatest physician in the Roman Empire was Galen. He was a Greek, but he lived in Rome. He became interested in medicine as a young boy. So he decided to become a doctor. He went to Alexandria to study medicine. After he became a doctor, he worked as a surgeon for gladiators. He learned a great deal by healing men wounded in the arena. Later, he moved to Rome. He became the personal doctor for Emperor Marcus Aurelius. Galen continued to study, too. He focused on anatomy. He learned a great deal about the human body through his studies. For instance, he learned about the functions of the kidneys. He also studied medicine. He even made a medicine called theriac. People used it until the 1800s.

1 ⓑ
2 ⓐ
3 ⓐ T ⓑ F ⓒ T

Unit 06 Nicholas Copernicus

p. 33

Pre-Listening Questions Sample Answer

1 I guess he is Nicholas Copernicus.
2 He lived hundreds of years ago. I don't know exactly when he lived.
3 He was an astronomer. That's all I know.

Vocabulary

1 orbit
2 Earth
3 solar system

p. 34

Script

W Teacher: People in the past were fascinated by the sun, moon, stars, and planets. The ancient Egyptians and Chinese studied them. So did people in other cultures. For example, the ancient Greeks loved astronomy. The great philosopher Aristotle wrote about the universe. He believed Earth was the center of the universe. He thought that everything else—the sun, moon, stars, and planets—orbited Earth. This was the geocentric model of the universe.

For centuries, most people thought Aristotle's version of the universe was true. Then, Nicholas Copernicus began to study astronomy. He lived from 1473 to 1543. He lived in the middle of the

Renaissance. It was a time of learning. People at that time were especially interested in knowledge from ancient Greece.

Copernicus read the works of Aristotle. Then, he tried to figure out mathematical calculations for the movements of the stars. Copernicus was good at math. But he couldn't get the math to work for Aristotle's model of the universe.

Copernicus came to believe that Aristotle had been wrong. So he made his own model of the universe. In his model, the sun was at the center of the solar system. Earth was the third planet from the sun. The moon orbited Earth. He put the other known planets—Mercury, Venus, Mars, Jupiter, and Saturn—in their correct orbits. This was the heliocentric model of the universe. Copernicus published his findings in his book *On the Revolutions of Heavenly Bodies* just before he died.

Organizer

ⓐ Aristotle
ⓑ center
ⓒ Earth
ⓓ Nicholas Copernicus
ⓔ solar system
ⓕ correct

p. 35

Comprehension

1 ⓐ 2 ⓐ 3 ⓒ
4 ⓒ 5 heliocentric model

6 ⓓ 7 ⓐ 8 ⓔ
9 ⓒ 10 ⓑ

p. 36

Listening Skills Practice: Details II

A ⓐ Chinese, astronomy
ⓑ Nicholas Copernicus, universe
ⓒ heliocentric model, Earth

B

Script

M Observatory Director: Thank you all for coming to the observatory. We're going to look at many objects tonight. One of them is Mars. Humans have known about Mars for thousands of years. But no one knew exactly how it orbited the sun until Johannes Kepler figured it out. Kepler was a German astronomer. He lived from 1571 to 1630. When he was alive, people were just realizing that the Earth was not the center of the universe. Instead, it—and the other planets—orbited the sun. Kepler studied the orbit of Mars for a long time. He saw that it didn't orbit the sun in a circle. Instead, it orbited the sun in an ellipse. An ellipse is shaped like an oval. This discovery was one of the three laws of planetary motion that Kepler discovered. He learned that every planet orbits the sun in an ellipse.

1 ⓑ
2 ⓑ
3 ⓐ T ⓑ F ⓒ F

Unit 07 Albert Einstein

p. 37

Pre-Listening Questions Sample Answer

1 He was a physicist.
2 He made a lot of great scientific discoveries.
3 I know about Stephen Hawking. He made some discoveries in physics. And Galileo Galilei was a great astronomer.

Vocabulary

1 professor
2 Nobel Prize
3 equation

p. 38

Script

M Teacher: On March 14, 1879, Albert Einstein was born. He would become one of the greatest scientists in history. When he was young, his teachers didn't believe he was special. In fact, he was just an average student. Einstein didn't enjoy many of the subjects he studied. But he did enjoy science and math a lot.

Einstein dropped out of school when he was fifteen. Later, he continued his studies. He finished his degree in 1900. Then, he took a job working at the patent office in Bern, Switzerland. During his free time, he studied physics. In 1905, he published a few papers. They were some of the most important scientific papers of the 1900s.

One of the papers concerned special relativity.

The other contained the famous equation E = mc^2. The equation describes how matter can be turned into energy. Thanks to those papers, people began to learn about Einstein. In 1910, he became a professor at the University of Zurich. In 1914, he moved to Berlin, Germany and took a job there.

In 1919, Einstein's theory of relativity was proven to be correct. This made him famous all around the world. In 1921, he received the Nobel Prize in Physics. He continued to work in Germany. But he left the country due to the political situation in 1932. He moved to the United States and started working there. He continued to do research on physics until he died on April 18, 1955.

Organizer

ⓐ subjects ⓑ patent
ⓒ correct ⓓ Physics
ⓔ Germany ⓕ Died

p. 39

Comprehension

1 ⓐ 2 ⓑ 3 ⓒ
4 ⓑ 5 scientists

6 ⓓ 7 ⓐ 8 ⓑ
9 ⓔ 10 ⓒ

p. 40

Listening Skills Practice: Sequencing I

A ⓐ 1 ⓑ 3 ⓒ 2

B

Script

M Teacher: In the 1930s, Germany started to build up its military. Adolf Hitler took power in the country. People all around the world feared there would be war. In 1939, Germany invaded Poland. This began World War II. Right before the war started, Albert Einstein wrote to U.S. President Franklin Roosevelt. He mentioned that it was possible to make an atomic bomb. Einstein believed Germany was trying to make its own atomic bomb. He wanted the U.S. to make one first. The U.S then started the Manhattan Project in 1941. That was the name of the American atomic bomb project. The greatest scientists in the country worked on the bomb in secret. They included Robert Oppenheimer, Enrico Fermi, Neils Bohr, and Richard Feynman. In 1945, they completed their task. They made an atomic bomb. On July 16, 1945, the first atomic bomb was detonated. The Atomic Age had begun.

1 ⓑ
2 ⓐ
3 ⓐ 2 ⓑ 3 ⓒ 1

Unit 08 Marie Curie

p. 41

Pre-Listening Questions Sample Answer

1 I'm not really sure. I think she studied chemistry though.
2 She lived around 100 years ago.
3 I know she won two Nobel Prizes.

Vocabulary

1 research project
2 X-ray machine
3 treatment

p. 42

Script

W Teacher: On November 7, 1867, Maria Sklodowska was born in Poland. Few people have ever heard of her. However, lots of people know her by her married name: Marie Curie. Marie Curie was one of the greatest scientists in the early twentieth century.

Marie wanted to become a scientist as a child. But she couldn't do that in her native Poland. So, in 1891, she moved to France. She went to a university there. Then, in 1894, she met Pierre Curie. He was a scientist, too. A year later, they got married. They did a number of research projects together.

Marie and Pierre did research on radiation. They made some new discoveries. In 1903, they were both awarded the Nobel Prize in Physics for their work on radiation. Unfortunately, in 1906, Pierre was involved in an accident and died. Marie was greatly upset by his death. But she continued her work in science.

In 1911, she received another Nobel Prize. This time, the award was in the field of chemistry. During her research, Marie discovered two new elements. They were polonium and radium. Thanks to her two Nobel Prizes, Marie became famous. Many scientists visited her and wanted to work with her.

Marie continued to work for the rest of her life. She helped invent a portable X-ray machine. She also realized that radiation could be helpful in the treatment of cancer. When she died in 1934, she was one of the most famous women in the world.

Organizer

ⓐ Poland ⓑ known
ⓒ married ⓓ radiation
ⓔ 1911 ⓕ portable

p. 43

Comprehension

1 ⓒ 2 ⓑ 3 ⓐ
4 ⓒ 5 Nobel Prize

6 ⓔ 7 ⓐ 8 ⓑ
9 ⓒ 10 ⓓ

p. 44

Listening Skills Practice: Sequencing II

A ⓐ 3 ⓑ 1 ⓒ 2

B

Script

M News Broadcaster: Yesterday, July 4, 1934, the famous scientist Marie Curie passed away. Born in 1867, Marie Curie worked hard in her youth to become a great scientist. She focused on the fields of physics and chemistry. She was so good at both of them that she won a Nobel Prize in each field. She won a Nobel Prize in Physics in 1903. And she got one in chemistry in 1911. She did much of her work on radiation. Unfortunately, it was likely radiation that killed her. During her research, Marie Curie was exposed to a lot of X-rays and other types of radiation. Since there were few studies on radiation in the early 1900s, no one knew how dangerous they were. So Curie—and others—didn't take any safety measures. We now know that radiation can be dangerous to people. And that is what caused Marie Curie's death.

1 ⓑ
2 ⓐ
3 ⓐ 1 ⓑ 3 ⓒ 2

Chapter 3 Historical Eras

Unit 09 The Stone Age

p. 47

Pre-Listening Questions Sample Answer

1 It was thousands of years ago.
2 I guess that people used stones for tools back then.
3 It was probably very difficult. There were no machines. In addition, the people then probably had very simple lives.

Vocabulary

1 ice age
2 humanoid
3 spear point

p. 48

Script

M Teacher: There have been many ages in history. Now, we live in the Modern Age. It's an advanced time. But today's technology is a fairly recent invention. For most of human history, people lived primitive lives. In fact, the longest period of time in human history is called the Stone Age. During it, humans mostly made tools with stones.

The Stone Age began around three million years ago. Then, modern humans didn't even exist. There were other humanoids alive though. Modern humans evolved from them later. These humanoids lived in Africa. They made simple tools from stone. For instance, they made stone weapons such as spear points. They made other tools from stones as well.

Scientists today divide the Stone Age into three separate periods. They are the Paleolithic, Mesolithic, and Neolithic periods. The Paleolithic Period started about three million years ago. It ended around 40,000 years ago. During it, humans were primitive hunter-gatherers. They used very simple stone tools.

The Mesolithic Period ended around 10,000 years ago. During it, humans had to survive the last major ice age. This period ended when humans discovered how to grow crops. It ended at different times in different places.

The Neolithic Period also ended at various times. For example, it lasted until 2000 B.C. in some places. This was the most advanced time in the Stone Age. Humans learned to tame some animals. They started farming as well. So they made permanent settlements. The first human towns and cities also arose during the Neolithic Period.

Organizer

ⓐ Paleolithic
ⓑ hunter-gathers
ⓒ 10,000
ⓓ Ended
ⓔ 2000
ⓕ permanent

p. 49

Comprehension

1 ⓑ
2 ⓐ
3 ⓑ
4 ⓐ
5 Mesolithic
6 ⓒ
7 ⓑ
8 ⓔ
9 ⓓ
10 ⓐ

p. 50

Listening Skills Practice: Understanding Organization I

A ⓐ ⓘⓘ ⓑ ⓘ

B

Script

W Teacher: After the Neolithic Period ended, a new period began. It was the Bronze Age. During it, humans learned to make metal tools from bronze. Bronze is an alloy. An alloy is a combination of two or more metals. Bronze is usually made of copper and tin. The Bronze Age began at different times in places around the world. For example, in Egypt and Mesopotamia, it started around 3300 B.C. It started at later times in other places though. The reason was that those civilizations were less advanced than the ones in Egypt and Mesopotamia. Writing systems were developed during the Bronze Age. Cities became larger. And people engaged in long-distance trade with members of other cultures. At the end of the Bronze Age, humans learned how to make iron tools. This ended the Bronze Age and started the Iron Age. That happened around 1000 B.C.

1 ⓑ
2 ⓐ
3 ⓒ

Unit 10 Ancient Greece

p. 51

Pre-Listening Questions Sample Answer

1 It's in Athens, Greece.

2 The ancient Greeks started Western civilization. They were the founders of democracy.

3 Plato and Socrates lived in ancient Greece. Alexander the Great was from that time. There were many other great people in ancient Greece. They were advanced in science and medicine as well.

Vocabulary

1 Olympic Games
2 Socrates
3 Alexander the Great

p. 52

Script

M Teacher: One of the most important ancient civilizations existed in Greece. Greece is located in Southeastern Europe. It lies on the shores of the northern part of the Mediterranean Sea. The ancient Greeks were the founders of Western civilization.

Ancient Greek civilization is divided into three separate periods. They are the Archaic, Classical, and Hellenistic periods. The Archaic Period lasted from around 800 B.C. to 508 B.C. During it, the poet Homer composed the epic poems the Iliad and the Odyssey. In addition, the first Olympic Games were held during this time.

During the Classical Period, the Greeks began to practice democracy. The Greeks also established city-states. These were large cities that ruled the land around them. The greatest Greek city-state was Athens. It produced many famous statesmen, scientists, philosophers, and warriors. Socrates and Plato, the great philosophers, lived during the Classical Period. Athens wasn't the only powerful city-state though. Thebes and Corinth were two others. Sparta was another. Athens and Sparta were great rivals. They fought each other in the Peloponnesian War. It was a long war that lasted from 431 to 404 B.C.

The Hellenistic Period began in 323 B.C. That was the year Alexander the Great died. Alexander and his armies conquered much of the known world. So Greek culture spread to many places. However, by 146 B.C., the Greeks had weakened while the Romans had become more powerful. The Romans conquered the Greeks in that year and brought an end to ancient Greece.

Organizer

ⓐ *Odyssey* ⓑ Classical
ⓒ city-states ⓓ Athens
ⓔ died ⓕ Greeks

p. 53

Comprehension

1 ⓐ 2 ⓑ 3 ⓒ
4 ⓑ 5 Western civilization

6 ⓑ 7 ⓐ 8 ⓔ
9 ⓒ 10 ⓓ

p. 54

Listening Skills Practice: Understanding Organization II

A ⓐ ⓘ ⓑ ⓘ

B

Script

M Tour Guide: Thanks for visiting Thermopylae. This was the site of one of history's most famous battles. In 480 B.C., King Xerxes of Persia invaded Greece. He had an army of 100,000 men. His army invaded Greece from the north. The Persians had to pass through Thermopylae to get to the rest of Greece. As you can see, it's a very narrow path. A tiny force of 300 Spartans blocked the path. It was 100,000 versus 300. But the Spartans didn't flee. They stayed and fought. In fact, when Xerxes saw the small Greek army facing him, he told the Spartans to drop their weapons. Leonidas, the Spartan king, responded by saying, "*Molon labe*." That's Greek for "come and take them." The Spartans held out for three days. Then, 299 of them were killed. The Spartans lost the battle, but the Persians returned to Asia. So the Greeks won the war.

1 ⓐ
2 ⓑ
3 ⓐ

Unit 11 The Middle Ages

p. 55

Pre-Listening Questions Sample Answer

1 It's a castle.
2 Kings and queens used to live in castles.
3 The Middle Ages were a few hundred years ago. Life in medieval times was simple. It was also difficult. People had hard lives.

Vocabulary

1 king
2 noble
3 serf

p. 56

Script

M Teacher: In 476, the Roman Empire fell. It was captured by Germanic barbarians. Yet Rome had been steadily losing power for many decades before 476. When the Roman Period ended, the Middle Ages began. The Middle Ages lasted from around 400 to 1500 in some places.

One major characteristic of the Middle Ages is that Europe wasn't unified. Previously, Rome had controlled much of Europe. But the Middle Ages featured many small independent kingdoms instead.

During the Middle Ages, lots of knowledge from Rome was lost. There had been many large urban areas in the Roman Empire. But life in medieval times revolved around smaller cities and towns. The Church became one of the most important parts of society. So it dominated most people's lives.

The Middle Ages was a violent period. Christian Europeans often had to defend against invading Muslims. Muslim armies conquered much of Spain. After that, they invaded France. But Charles Martel defeated them at the Battle of Tours in 732. Centuries later, the Europeans launched the Crusades. They were a series of wars in the Middle East. The Europeans were trying to drive the Muslims out of Jerusalem and the land around it.

In many places, the system of government was feudalism. The king was at the top of this system. Beneath him were his nobles. The king granted the nobles land. They provided him with soldiers and taxes. Beneath the nobles were serfs. They farmed the land for the nobles. The serfs' lives were very difficult.

Organizer

ⓐ 1500 ⓑ Rome
ⓒ violent ⓓ Muslims
ⓔ Power ⓕ difficult

p. 57

Comprehension

1 ⓒ 2 ⓑ 3 ⓐ
4 ⓐ 5 Crusades
6 ⓒ 7 ⓔ 8 ⓓ
9 ⓑ 10 ⓐ

p. 58

Listening Skills Practice: Connecting Words I

A ⓐ But
ⓑ So
ⓒ After that

B

Script

M Teacher: In 1328, some people in China started getting sick. They got black spots all over their bodies. Then, they died. This disease was the bubonic plague. It was contagious, so it slowly spread. It began making its way west along the Silk Road. In 1347, it arrived in Europe. From 1347 to 1350, people in Europe suffered through a time they called the Black Death. Millions of people died. Somewhere from thirty to fifty percent of all Europeans died. It was a terrible period. However, there were some positive results after the Black Death ended. With fewer people, there was more food for the survivors. Therefore, they ate better and became healthier. Laborers were paid more for their work, so people became richer. And many survivors lost faith in the Church. They started studying fields other than religion. This helped lead to the Renaissance in the 1400s.

1 ⓑ
2 ⓑ
3 ⓐ so ⓑ But ⓒ and

Unit 12 The Renaissance

p. 59

Pre-Listening Questions Sample Answer

1 There is a statue. I think it's called *David*. And there is a picture by Leonardo da Vinci. I don't know the name though.
2 I think it started in Italy.
3 Leonardo da Vinci lived during the Renaissance. He was an artist, engineer, and scientist. Michelangelo lived then, too. He was a great artist.

Vocabulary

1 threaten
2 scholar
3 text

p. 60

Script

W Teacher: In the 1300s, the Byzantine Empire was in decline. The Ottoman Turks were attacking it from the east and threatening it. As a result, many Byzantines fled the empire. Lots of them moved west and went to Italy. Many of these people were scholars. They brought texts from ancient Greece and Rome with them. These texts had been lost in the West. The Byzantines reintroduced them. This helped start the Renaissance in Europe around 1400.

The word Renaissance means "rebirth." This was a period when there was a rebirth in knowledge. Thanks to the texts from ancient times, the Europeans were able to relearn lost knowledge from the past. The Renaissance began in the Italian city-state of Florence. Then, it spread to other places in Italy, such as Rome and Venice. Next, it made its way north to France, the Germanic states, England, the Netherlands, and other places.

One primary feature of the Renaissance was humanism. It was a new way of thinking. Humanists believed that everyone should be educated. They also wanted people to learn about the arts, science, and literature. Humanism dramatically affected how people thought during this period.

There were many advances during the Renaissance. There were improvements in art, science, engineering, and other fields. There were lots of brilliant men as well. Some of them were so great that they were called Renaissance Men. A Renaissance Man was someone who excelled in several fields. Leonardo da Vinci and Michelangelo Buonarroti were two such people.

Organizer

ⓐ texts ⓑ Italy
ⓒ humanism ⓓ literature
ⓔ many ⓕ art

p. 61

Comprehension

1 ⓒ 2 ⓒ 3 ⓐ
4 ⓑ 5 Byzantine

6 ⓓ 7 ⓐ 8 ⓒ
9 ⓔ 10 ⓑ

p. 62

Listening Skills Practice: Connecting Words II

A ⓐ such as
ⓑ when
ⓒ and

B

Script

W Art Gallery Director: I'm glad to announce that we have a new exhibit opening today. It has some of the best art from the Renaissance. Renaissance art was very different from medieval art. Most medieval art had religion as a topic. Renaissance artists made religious works as well. But they also painted scenes from mythology and history. Many of them used realism in their artwork. They used many new techniques. Two of them were perspective and proportion. They often used light and dark colors in their art. This exhibit focuses on the works of Italian masters from this time. We have works by Leonardo da Vinci, Michelangelo, and Botticelli. We also have some paintings by Caravaggio, Raphael, and Titian. You're going to love the collection we have put together. Now, please follow me, and I'll tell you about each painting. The first one we're going to see is by Botticelli.

1 ⓒ
2 ⓒ
3 ⓐ but ⓑ and ⓒ and

Chapter 4 Landmarks

Unit 13 The Eiffel Tower

p. 65

Pre-Listening Questions Sample Answer

1 It's in Paris, France.
2 It was built in the 1800s.
3 In Korea, the 63 Building is a famous landmark. Namdaemun is another famous landmark. And the statue of Admiral Lee Sunshin is a well-known landmark.

Vocabulary

1 debate
2 radio tower
3 elevator

p. 66

Script

W Teacher: In 1889, the city of Paris, France, was going to host the World's Fair. This was considered a major event. So the organizers wanted to impress people around the world. They decided to erect an imposing building. A contest was held. A design for an enormous tower was selected as the winner. Construction began in 1887. On March 31, 1889, the Eiffel Tower was complete.

The Eiffel Tower rose 324 meters high. When it was finished, it was the highest manmade structure in the world. It remained the highest building until 1930. The Eiffel Tower was built with several thousand tons of iron. It had an elevator which took people up to the top. There, they could see nearly sixty kilometers on a cloudy day.

Even though the Eiffel Tower was unique, many Parisians in the 1800s hated it. They called it an eyesore. Lots of people believed it ruined the Paris skyline.

Originally, the plan was to let the Eiffel Tower remain standing for twenty years. Then, the tower would be torn down. However, because of its great height, the French started to use it as a radio tower. When the twenty-year period came, there was a debate. They decided not to tear down the tower.

Over time, the people of Paris changed their minds about the Eiffel Tower. Today, the Eiffel Tower is a symbol of Paris. It's beloved by the people of the city. And it's one of the most popular places with tourists in Paris.

Organizer

ⓐ 1889 ⓑ manmade
ⓒ hated ⓓ twenty
ⓔ radio tower ⓕ Paris

p. 67

Comprehension

1 ⓑ 2 ⓑ 3 ⓒ
4 ⓑ 5 symbol

6 ⓒ 7 ⓓ 8 ⓔ
9 ⓑ 10 ⓐ

p. 68

Listening Skills Practice: Guessing Unknown Words I

A ⓐ

B

Script

M Teacher: It's difficult to make too many positive comments about George Washington. He led the Americans to victory in the Revolutionary War. He was the first president of the United States. And he is called "The Father of His Country," too. Washington died in 1799. After his death, many Americans wanted to build a monument for him. But they couldn't agree on what to do. Finally, in 1848, construction on a monument in Washington, D.C. began. The project moved slowly, and it actually stopped in 1854. Construction began again in 1878. In 1884, the Washington Monument was completed. It was a giant obelisk that stood 555 feet high. So it's a tall, narrow tower. It was 55 feet around at the bottom. From the top of the Washington Monument, visitors can see the entire city of Washington, D.C. as well as much of the surrounding area.

1 ⓒ
2 ⓐ
3 ⓐ

Unit 14 The Leaning Tower of Pisa

p. 69

Pre-Listening Questions Sample Answer

1 It's in Pisa, Italy.
2 I'm not sure. I guess it's really heavy. And the builders probably did a bad job.
3 Lots of people like taking pictures of it. They try to look like they are holding it up.

Vocabulary

1 cathedral
2 bell
3 construction

p. 70

Script

W Teacher: Many of the world's most famous buildings are quite tall. But there's a tower in Italy that isn't very tall. As a matter of fact, it's only around fifty-six meters tall. This building is renowned for another reason: It leans to one side. It's the Leaning Tower of Pisa.

In the Middle Ages, the city of Pisa had a cathedral. The cathedral needed a bell tower. So in 1173, construction on the bell tower began. Unfortunately, the builders were very inexperienced. They didn't realize they were building the tower on unsuitable ground. As a result, the building started to lean to one side. This happened during the first stage of construction of the tower. That stage ended in 1178. By then, the builders had erected three floors.

Construction on the tower didn't start again until 1275. This was the second stage. It ended with three more floors being built. The third stage added two more floors. It ended in 1350. Despite all of the work on the tower, it continued leaning.

Over the years, there have been several attempts to stop the tower from leaning. They have all failed though. Yet engineers have prevented the tower from falling over. Currently, the tower is considered stable and isn't in any danger of falling over.

The fact that the tower leans so much has actually increased its fame. It's one of the most recognizable buildings in the world simply because it doesn't stand up straight.

Organizer

ⓐ cathedral ⓑ first
ⓒ three ⓓ failed
ⓔ falling over ⓕ famous

p. 71

Comprehension

1 ⓒ 2 ⓐ 3 ⓑ
4 ⓐ 5 inexperienced

6 ⓓ 7 ⓑ 8 ⓐ
9 ⓔ 10 ⓒ

p. 72

Listening Skills Practice: Guessing Unknown Words II

A ⓑ

B

Script

M Tourist: Hi, Mary. It's Eric. You won't believe where I'm calling you from. I'm in Rome, Italy, on a trip with my family right now. We went on a tour of the city today and saw lots of amazing sights. For me, the Colosseum was my favorite place. It was built nearly 2,000 years ago. It's a giant stadium that had four different levels. It could hold around 50,000 people at one time. Today, parts of it have been destroyed. It must have been really impressive in the past. There used to be all sorts of games and activities held in the Colosseum. Lots of gladiators faught there, too. Even the emperor used to attend gladiator matches in the Colosseum. Well, I have to go now. I'll call you when I get back home. Bye.

1 ⓐ
2 ⓑ
3 ⓑ

Unit 15 The Taj Mahal

p. 73

Pre-Listening Questions Sample Answer

1 It's somewhere in India. I don't know the name of the city.
2 I think someone is buried there. I don't know who though.
3 The Louvre in Paris is a famous building. The Kremlin in Russia is famous, too. And Buckingham Palace in England is very famous.

Vocabulary

1 tomb
2 builder
3 precious metals

p. 74

Script

M Teacher: People will do all sorts of things for love. One man loved his wife so much that he had one of the most beautiful buildings on the Earth made in her honor. This building is the Taj Mahal.

In 1622, Shah Jahan became the emperor of the Mughal Empire in India. His third wife's name was Mumtaz Mahal. She was his favorite wife. In eighteen years of marriage, she gave birth to fourteen children. Sadly, when she was thirty-nine years old, she died while giving birth to her last child. Shah Jahan was devastated by her death. He ordered the Taj Mahal built to provide her with a fitting tomb.

Three architects designed the building together. Then, builders were imported from all over the Islamic world. For example, they came from Baghdad, Constantinople, and other places. More than 20,000 men worked on the Taj Mahal. They labored from 1632 to 1653. When they finished, they had truly created "the crown of palaces." That's what the name Taj Mahal means in English.

The Taj Mahal was made of white marble. Precious metals and gems were used as well. The Taj Mahal even appears to change colors throughout the day. In fact, in the morning, it looks pink. In the afternoon, it looks white. And in the evening, it looks golden.

Today, both the emperor and his wife are buried there. And millions of people visit the Taj Mahal each year to see the result of one man's love for his wife.

Organizer

ⓐ honor ⓑ favorite
ⓒ tomb ⓓ 20,000
ⓔ precious ⓕ throughout

p. 75

Comprehension

1 ⓐ 2 ⓒ 3 ⓐ
4 ⓑ 5 wife

6 ⓓ 7 ⓐ 8 ⓒ
9 ⓔ 10 ⓑ

p. 76

Listening Skills Practice: Supporting Details I

A ⓐ as well
ⓑ For example
ⓒ In fact

B

Script

W Teacher: *One building that people all around the world often recognize is in Sydney, Australia. It's the Sydney Opera House. It sits alongside Sydney Harbor. In addition, it's near the Sydney Harbor Bridge. The Sydney Opera House hosts around 3,000 events every year. But most people aren't interested in the events held at the opera house. Instead, they're more interested in its unique design. For example, the opera house has many shells made of tile. These shells rise high above the building. They remind people of the sails of the ships on the water in Sydney Harbor. John Utzon made the original design of the opera house. But his plans were too advanced for the technology of his time. As a result, there were many delays in its construction. Yet the Sydney Opera House was finally completed. Then, it opened in 1973.*

1 ⓒ
2 ⓐ
3 ⓐ ⓘⓘ ⓑ ⓘⓘⓘ ⓒ ⓘ

Unit 16 The Statue of Liberty

p. 77

Pre-Listening Questions Sample Answer

1 It's in New York City in the United States.
2 It represents liberty.
3 In Korea, the statue of Admiral Lee Sunshin is famous. *David* is a famous statue by Michelangelo. *The Thinker* is another famous statue.

Vocabulary

1 crown
2 chain
3 tablet

p. 78

Script

M Teacher: *One of the easiest statues to recognize in the entire world is in New York City. It's on Liberty Island, which is in New York Harbor. Its name is the Statue of Liberty.*

On July 4, 1776, the Americans declared their independence from England. They did this by signing the Declaration of Independence. The Americans also fought a war of freedom against England. It lasted from 1775 to 1783. During the Revolutionary War, France was an ally of the Americans.

In 1876, the Americans were celebrating 100 years of freedom. The French wanted to give a gift to the Americans. French sculptor Frederic Bartholdi was selected to design a statue. He came up with the idea of the Statue of Liberty. He based his design on Libertas. She was the Roman goddess of liberty. She is a symbol of freedom. She's holding a torch in her right hand. In her left hand, she's holding a tablet. On the tablet is the date of the signing of the Declaration of Independence. She's wearing a crown with seven spikes. And there's a broken chain on the ground at her feet.

The French weren't able to deliver the statue by 1876 though. Instead, the project ran into funding problems. Finally, both the pedestal—the base of the statue—and the statue itself were complete. The statue was dedicated on October 28, 1886. Since then, it has greeted everyone—both Americans and foreigners—who goes through New York Harbor to enter the United States.

Organizer

ⓐ England ⓑ gift
ⓒ goddess ⓓ symbol
ⓔ feet ⓕ Liberty

p. 79

Comprehension

1 ⓐ 2 ⓒ 3 ⓑ
4 ⓑ 5 Liberty Island

6 ⓒ 7 ⓐ 8 ⓑ
9 ⓔ 10 ⓓ

p. 80

Listening Skills Practice: Supporting Details II

A ⓐ SD ⓑ MI ⓒ SD

B

Script

M Guest Speaker: Hello, students. My name is Walter Schnell. I immigrated to the United States in 1938. That was a long time ago. I was just a young boy when I came here with my family. Still, I remember that trip very well. My family came from Germany. We took a ship all the way across the Atlantic Ocean. And then we arrived in New York Harbor. Everyone in my family was nervous at that time. We were moving to a new land. We had to visit Ellis Island first. That was an island in New York Harbor. Immigrants to the United States often went to Ellis Island before they could go onto land. But, before we went there, we saw another sight: the Statue of Liberty. She stood in the harbor and seemed to greet all of us. Once we saw her, we knew everything would be fine in our new country.

1 ⓑ
2 ⓒ
3 ⓐ Atlantic Ocean
ⓑ Ellis Island
ⓒ Statue of Liberty

Chapter 5 The Ocean

Unit 17 Coral Reefs

p. 83

Pre-Listening Questions Sample Answer

1 I can see some fish. And there is lots of different-colored coral in the picture.
2 They are located in tropical areas. They always grow in warm water.
3 I think coral reefs have lots of food. So the animals don't have to worry about finding food.

Vocabulary

1 shelter
2 marine biologist
3 sea creature

p. 84

Script

W Teacher: Coral reefs are some of the most vital ecosystems on the planet. They exist in a limited number of places though. The reason is that they can only survive in warm water. Coral reefs thrive in water that's between sixteen and thirty degrees Celsius. And they also exist only in shallow water. As a result, only about 0.2 percent of the bottom of the ocean is covered with coral.

Still, despite covering a tiny area, coral reefs provide food and shelter for thousands of aquatic species. In fact, marine biologists estimate that around twenty-five percent of all ocean animals live in or around coral reefs.

Most coral reefs are fairly small in size. Yet some can be vast. For instance, the Great Barrier Reef near Australia is enormous. It's a system that contains more than 3,000 coral reefs. It's about 2,500 kilometers long.

Coral reefs are important to animals for several reasons. First, the hard corals provide numerous hiding places for small fish. These let the fish evade predators. In fact, most large predators cannot even swim in coral reefs since the hard corals would cut them. Many fish—and other animals—also lay their eggs in coral reefs. When the eggs hatch, the fish can grow up in relative safety. Finally, coral reefs are rich in nutrients. So the animals living in them have a constant supply of food. These features make coral reefs attractive places to live for many sea creatures.

Organizer

ⓐ ecosystems ⓑ 30
ⓒ Only ⓓ small
ⓔ eggs ⓕ food

p. 85

Comprehension

1 ⓐ 2 ⓒ 3 ⓑ
4 ⓐ 5 aquatic species

6 ⓓ 7 ⓒ 8 ⓐ
9 ⓑ 10 ⓔ

p. 86

Listening Skills Practice: Dictation I

A ⓐ they can only survive in warm water
ⓑ between sixteen and thirty degrees Celsius
ⓒ only about 0.2 percent of the bottom of the ocean

B

Script

W Teacher: The Hawaiian island of Oahu is popular with tourists. It has many beautiful sights to see. One of the most popular places in Oahu is Hanauma Bay. The bay is fairly small. It's located in the crater of an extinct volcano. Today, there's a coral reef in the bay. More than 450 species of tropical fish live in the reef. Other aquatic animals live there as well. These include sea turtles and eels. Today, Hanauma Bay is a nature preserve. The government of Hawaii wants to keep it as a natural resource. Large numbers of tourists visit it every day. They can swim in the reef. They can go snorkeling there, too. But they can't do other activities, such as fishing and boating. By banning those activities, the coral reef can be preserved. Thus future generations will be able to enjoy it.

1 ⓐ
2 ⓒ
3 ⓐ places in Oahu is Hanauma Bay
ⓑ sea turtles and eels
ⓒ the coral reef can be preserved

Unit 18 The Mariana Trench

p. 87

Pre-Listening Questions Sample Answer

1 It looks pretty deep underwater. I don't know how deep though.
2 It's somewhere in the Pacific Ocean.
3 It must be very dark there. There are probably some animals like lobsters and crabs that live on the bottom of it.

Vocabulary

1 submersible
2 survey
3 tin can

p. 88

Script

M Teacher: Guam is an island in the northwest part of the Pacific Ocean. It lies south of Japan and east of the Philippines. Around 330 kilometers southwest of Guam is the Mariana Trench. This is the deepest place in the world's oceans. It descends at least 10,900 meters below sea level.

The Mariana Trench was first surveyed in 1951. A British ship named the *Challenger II* discovered the deepest part of the trench. The crew named the area Challenger Deep. Since that time, many other ships have surveyed the area. They learned that it's more than 2,500 kilometers long. It also has an average width of nearly seventy kilometers.

Because the trench is so deep, humans couldn't explore the bottom of it for many years. The reason concerns water pressure. Thousands of meters beneath the surface, the water pressure is so great that no human can survive. In fact, the water pressure would crush a submarine like it's a tin can. However, in recent years, highly advanced submersibles have been able to reach the bottom of the Mariana Trench.

These vehicles brought back valuable—and surprising—information. For instance, there are many hot-water vents in the trench. Most of the water there is very cold. Yet the vents provide pockets of hot water. That lets tiny animals called microbes live there. There are even some fish living there. Scientists had previously thought that no life could survive that deep. But there's an abundance of life in the Mariana Trench.

Organizer

ⓐ Pacific ⓑ east
ⓒ below ⓓ deepest
ⓔ explore ⓕ Water pressure

p. 89

Comprehension

1 ⓐ 2 ⓒ 3 ⓐ
4 ⓑ 5 Guam
6 ⓑ 7 ⓐ 8 ⓓ
9 ⓔ 10 ⓒ

p. 90

Listening Skills Practice: Dictation II

A ⓐ discovered the deepest part of the trench
ⓑ many other ships have surveyed the area
ⓒ an average width of nearly seventy kilometers

B

Script

W Newscaster: Most people know James Cameron for his movies. He directed *Avatar* and *Titanic*. They made more money than every other movie in history. But James Cameron has another interest: the ocean. On March 26, 2012, he made history in the ocean. He made a solo dive to the bottom of the Mariana Trench. He was the first person to do that. He went to the bottom of the ocean in a deep-sea submersible. It was called the *Deepsea Challenger*. Cameron explored the ocean floor while he was down there. He even conducted some science. For instance, he discovered more than sixty new species of animals. Most of them were bacteria. But he also found some animals that were similar to shrimp. Tonight, James Cameron is going to tell us all about his trip to the bottom of the ocean. Let's welcome James Cameron to our show.

1 ⓑ
2 ⓐ
3 ⓐ than every other movie in history
ⓑ in a deep-sea submersible
ⓒ more than sixty new species of animals

Unit 19 Deep-Sea Creatures

p. 91

Pre-Listening Questions Sample Answer

1 I guess they must live deep under the water.
2 The animal on the left seems to be glowing. I think it can make its own light. I don't know about the other animals though.
3 I imagine the animals must be strong to live there. The water deep beneath the sea is very cold.

Vocabulary

1 coelacanth
2 anglerfish
3 shallow

p. 92

Script

M Teacher: Near shore, the oceans are shallow. However, a few kilometers off shore, they become incredibly deep. In many places, the oceans are several kilometers deep. No sunlight can reach that deep beneath the surface. In addition, the conditions are harsh. The water is quite cold. The water pressure is intense. And there are few resources for fish. Nevertheless, many animals live deep beneath the surface of the ocean. We call them deep-sea creatures.

There are numerous types of bacteria that live deep underwater. But fish live there, too. There are several types of fish. Two are living fossils and fish that use bioluminescence.

Living fossils are fish that have been on the Earth for millions of years yet have barely evolved. The coelacanth is a living fossil. It was alive more than sixty-five million years ago when the dinosaurs were alive. In fact, scientists have found coelacanth fossils 350 million years old. The coelacanth has changed little during that time. The frilled shark is another living fossil. It lives more than 1,500 meters beneath the surface. It resembles the frilled sharks that lived millions of years ago.

Other deep-sea creature use bioluminescence. This means they can create their own light. Deep underwater, the sea is dark. So these animals evolved to be able to make their own light. The anglerfish can create light. It uses the light to attract other fish. Then, it catches and eats them. The lanternfish and giant flashlight fish can both make light, too.

Organizer

ⓐ millions ⓑ dinosaurs
ⓒ little ⓓ dark
ⓔ giant flashlight fish ⓕ attract

p. 93

Comprehension

1 ⓒ 2 ⓐ 3 ⓒ
4 ⓑ 5 fish

6 ⓒ 7 ⓐ 8 ⓑ
9 ⓔ 10 ⓓ

p. 94

Listening Skills Practice: Classification I

A ⓐ million
ⓑ evolved
ⓒ Resembles
ⓓ light
ⓔ dark
ⓕ Anglerfish

B

Script

W Teacher: *Life exists in some unusual places on Earth. For instance, animals can survive at the bottom of the sea. They live in the hottest deserts and the coldest places on the planet, too. There is even life that survives high above the planet's surface. The stratosphere is one layer of the atmosphere. It's around ten to fifty kilometers above the ground. No large animals can live there. But small ones can. These creatures are called microbes. Microbes are extremely small. You need a microscope to see them. They include bacteria, fungi, and viruses. They all live in great numbers in the stratosphere. Some of these microbes are harmful to humans. Scientists have discovered several dangerous viruses living high above the Earth's surface. They don't know how the microbes can survive up there yet. But they're doing research to learn why.*

1 ⓐ
2 ⓒ
3 ⓐ small
ⓑ bacteria
ⓒ stratosphere
ⓓ harmful
ⓔ Scientists

Unit 20 Sharks

p. 95

Pre-Listening Questions Sample Answer

1 It looks like a great white shark.
2 There are hammerhead sharks. Tiger sharks, whale sharks, and nurse sharks are three other kinds of sharks.
3 They sometimes attack humans. But most shark species leave humans alone.

Vocabulary

1 scuba diving
2 shark attack
3 tiger shark

p. 96

Script

W Teacher: *In 1975, the movie Jaws came out. It told the story of a man-eating shark that was attacking people. After watching the movie, millions of people were afraid to go into the water. They shouldn't have been. Worldwide, there are only about 100 shark attacks per year. And fewer than twenty people die from shark attacks each year.*

There are hundreds of species of sharks. Most of them aren't man-eaters. Yet there are a few sharks that do attack humans. The three most common of them are great white sharks, tiger sharks, and bull sharks. They're responsible for nearly all shark attacks on humans.

Great white sharks are the most fearsome creatures in the ocean. They can grow up to eight meters long and weigh more than three tons. They have 3,000 teeth and attack their prey by biting it. They often swim near the shore. Great whites account for around half of all shark attacks each year.

Tiger sharks are smaller than great whites. They grow to be around five meters in length. They live in tropical waters. They're dangerous to people who enjoy scuba diving and swimming in places such as Hawaii.

Bull sharks are slightly more than two meters long. But they're very dangerous. They often swim close to shore. They even swim in fresh water sometimes. They can swim in water less than one meter deep. They're also really aggressive, so they sometimes attack people who are close to shore.

Organizer

ⓐ 100
ⓑ Kill
ⓒ not
ⓓ 3 tons
ⓔ tropical
ⓕ aggressive

p. 97

Comprehension

1 ⓑ 2 ⓒ 3 ⓑ

4 ⓑ

5 man-eating sharks

6 ⓑ

7 ⓔ

8 ⓓ

9 ⓐ

10 ⓒ

p. 98

Listening Skills Practice: Classification II

A ⓐ 3,000
ⓑ half
ⓒ 5 meters
ⓓ tropical
ⓔ dangerous
ⓕ aggressive

B

Script

M Reporter: There was a shark attack at a beach near Honolulu, Hawaii, today. According to witnesses, a woman was swimming about fifty meters from shore. Then, a large shark suddenly attacked her. A man swimming near the woman saw the shark attack. He swam toward the woman. Apparently, he hit the shark on the tip of its nose several times. This caused the shark to let go of the woman. Then, it swam away. The man acted properly. There are several things to do in case a shark attacks you. You can hit it in the eyes, gills, or nose. You should also stay calm. Don't wave your arms around in the water. That will make the shark attack even more. Don't try to swim faster than the shark. That's impossible. But try to get out of the water as quickly as possible.

1 ⓑ

2 ⓐ

3 ⓐ eyes
ⓑ calm
ⓒ arms
ⓓ swim
ⓔ water

Word List

Word List

Chapter 1 Amazing Places

Unit 01

1 **breathtaking** *(adj)* wonderful; incredible; amazing
The view of the Earth from outer space is ***breathtaking***.

2 **canopy** *(n)* a covering
Animals such as monkeys live in the jungle ***canopy***.

3 **connect** *(v)* to join
Try to ***connect*** the two pieces to each other.

4 **diverse** *(adj)* varied; different
A ***diverse*** amount of animals live in this region.

5 **drop** *(n)* a decline
There was a sudden ***drop*** in the air pressure yesterday.

6 **include** *(v)* to consist of; to take in
The cost of the trip ***includes*** airfare and hotel rooms.

7 **remarkable** *(adj)* incredible; significant
It was ***remarkable*** how the team was able to win the game.

8 **rise** *(v)* to go up
The temperature will ***rise*** as the sun gets higher in the sky.

9 **tourist** *(n)* a person who visits a place for sightseeing
Some of the ***tourists*** are going to go to the palace now.

10 **waterfall** *(n)* a place where water drops to a lower level
This is one of the most beautiful ***waterfalls*** in the area.

Unit 02

1 **calm** *(adj)* quiet; peaceful; not loud or upset
Please stay ***calm*** and try not to make any noise at all.

2 **entire** *(adj)* complete; total
Everyone on the tour enjoyed the ***entire*** trip.

3 **experience** *(v)* to undergo
You will ***experience*** the time of your life if you go there.

4 **fascinating** *(adj)* impressive; amazing; incredible
It is ***fascinating*** to go scuba diving in the ocean.

5 **flat** *(adj)* level; even
The land in this region is very ***flat*** with no hills.

6 **flow** *(v)* to move, as in a liquid
Water ***flows*** from high levels to lower ones.

7 **hike** *(v)* to walk a long distance
We plan to ***hike*** through the forest for the entire day.

8 **rapids** *(n)* white water; water that moves quickly, often over rocks
They enjoyed rafting in the ***rapids*** of that river.

9 **ruins** *(n)* the remains of an old building
You can see many ***ruins*** of ancient buildings in Greece.

10 **view** *(n)* a look; a sight
The ***view*** from the top of the mountain is incredible.

Unit 03

1 **continent** *(n)* one of the seven large landmasses on the Earth
The biggest ***continent*** on the Earth is Asia.

2 **cross** *(v)* to go across or over something
We can ***cross*** the river at the bridge to the north.

3 **follow** *(v)* to go after

We are going to ***follow*** him to his office.

4 **geography** *(n)* the study of the Earth's surface

You can learn about many landforms by studying ***geography***.

5 **grassland** *(n)* an area that has many grasses and bushes but few trees

There are some cows and sheep on the ***grassland***.

6 **herbivore** *(n)* an animal that only eats vegetation

Zebras are large ***herbivores*** that live in Africa.

7 **migrate** *(v)* to move from one area to another, often for a long period of time

Many birds ***migrate*** south when the weather gets cold.

8 **plain** *(n)* a large area of land that is flat

The ***plain*** extends as far as the eye can see.

9 **survive** *(v)* to stay alive; to keep from dying

The people in that warzone hope to ***survive*** the fighting.

10 **vicious** *(adj)* violent

Mother bears can be ***vicious*** animals if their cubs are in danger.

Unit 04

1 **float** *(v)* to stay on the surface of a liquid such as water

Karen is using a life preserver to ***float*** on the water.

2 **heal** *(v)* to get better physically; to improve one's physical condition

The medicine ***healed*** Jim very quickly.

3 **instantly** *(adv)* at once; immediately

Instantly, Sarah thought of the correct answer.

4 **physical** *(adj)* relating to the body

How is your ***physical*** condition these days?

5 **plateau** *(n)* a flat area of land that is higher than the land around it

There is a large ***plateau*** in the western part of the United States.

6 **remain** *(v)* to stay in a certain place

Try to ***remain*** in the same place until I get back.

7 **sail** *(v)* to move like a boat or ship

We enjoy ***sailing*** on the lake on the weekend.

8 **salty** *(adj)* having a large amount of salt

The water in the ocean is too ***salty*** to drink.

9 **snorkel** *(v)* to swim while using a breathing device called a snorkel

You can go ***snorkeling*** in the coral reef.

10 **surface** *(n)* the top level of water or another liquid

The ***surface*** of the water is covered with a lot of algae.

Chapter 2 Great Scientists

Unit 05

1 **anatomy** *(n)* the structure of the body; the study of the structure of the body

We learned a great deal by studying ***anatomy***.

2 **care** *(v)* to be interested in; to be concerned about

I do not ***care*** what happens later on.

3 **function** *(n)* a purpose; a use; a role

How many ***functions*** does your smartphone have?

4 **gladiator** *(n)* a person in ancient Rome who fought others for entertainment

Some ***gladiators*** fought lions and tigers instead of other men.

5 **graduate** *(v)* to complete a course of study at a school
Jane is going to ***graduate*** from college next year.

6 **illness** *(n)* a sickness
Doctors do not yet know what kind of ***illness*** Sue has.

7 **myth** *(n)* a story from the past that may or may not be true; a legend
There are many ***myths*** from ancient Greece for you to read.

8 **surgeon** *(n)* a doctor that performs operations
The ***surgeon*** will operate on the patient for about two hours.

9 **treat** *(v)* to take care of a person's health
Doctors are able to ***treat*** some patients with cancer these days.

10 **tremendous** *(adj)* enormous; very big
It took a ***tremendous*** amount of courage to run into the burning building.

Unit 06

1 **astronomy** *(n)* the study of outer space and everything in it
Greg wants to study ***astronomy*** at his university.

2 **correct** *(adj)* right; proper
Try to solve the problem and to get the ***correct*** answer.

3 **ellipse** *(n)* a closed object shaped like an oval
The orbit of every planet in the solar system is an ***ellipse***.

4 **finding** *(n)* a discovery
The professor will talk about his ***finding*** tonight.

5 **observatory** *(n)* a place where people observe the night sky
The ***observatory*** has a very large telescope.

6 **orbit** *(v)* to move around something repeatedly in a circle
It takes 365 days for Earth to ***orbit*** the sun.

7 **philosopher** *(n)* a person who studies wisdom
Socrates was a famous ***philosopher*** from ancient Greece.

8 **planetary** *(adj)* relating to a planet
Mr. Taylor is studying the ***planetary*** atmosphere of Venus.

9 **publish** *(v)* to print a book, article, or something similar
The company is going to ***publish*** the book next week.

10 **realize** *(v)* to recognize; to understand
You need to ***realize*** that you have to try harder.

Unit 07

1 **complete** *(v)* to finish
You need to ***complete*** your work by this Friday.

2 **concern** *(v)* to be about
Amy's speech ***concerns*** the recent cold weather.

3 **detonate** *(v)* to explode
The bomb ***detonated*** and destroyed the building.

4 **equation** *(n)* a math problem
The teacher wrote the difficult ***equation*** on the board.

5 **invade** *(v)* to enter a new territory and to attack the people there
The country is planning to ***invade*** its neighbor soon.

6 **mention** *(v)* to state; to say
Nobody ***mentioned*** any special rules to follow.

7 **military** *(n)* an army; armed forces
That country's ***military*** is not very powerful.

8 **prove** *(v)* to show that something is right
Peter will ***prove*** that he did not steal the money.

9 **scientist** *(n)* a person who studies science
These days, many ***scientists*** are not very honest.

10 **task** *(n)* a job; a chore; a duty
I have three more ***tasks*** to do by six o'clock.

Unit 08

1 **discover** *(v)* to find something new
They are hoping to ***discover*** gold in that area.

2 **invent** *(v)* to make something new
The engineer is trying to ***invent*** a new type of computer.

3 **likely** *(adv)* probably
It is ***likely*** that we will win the game.

4 **measure** *(n)* an act; an action
They took some ***measures*** to protect themselves.

5 **prize** *(n)* an award
Jonathan won the grand ***prize*** at the art contest.

6 **receive** *(v)* to win; to get
You will ***receive*** some money if you win an award.

7 **safety** *(adj)* security; protective
Please wear your ***safety*** vest at all times.

8 **unfortunately** *(adv)* sadly; unhappily
Unfortunately, I have to cancel our meeting this afternoon.

9 **upset** *(adj)* sad; disappointed; hurt
Helen was ***upset*** when she heard the bad news.

10 **youth** *(n)* a young age; a young person
What did you enjoy doing in your ***youth***?

Chapter 3 Historical Eras

Unit 09

1 **alloy** *(n)* a metal made from a combination of two or more metals
Bronze was one of the first ***alloys*** humans ever made.

2 **arise** *(v)* to start; to appear
Human civilization first ***arose*** thousands of years ago.

3 **crop** *(n)* a plant grown by a farmer, often in great amounts
Rice and wheat are two common ***crops*** in this country.

4 **humanoid** *(n)* a creature that is like a human but is somewhat different
Millions of years ago, some ***humanoids*** lived on the Earth.

5 **modern** *(adj)* advanced; from the present time
In ***modern*** times, many people know how to use computers.

6 **primitive** *(adj)* simple; basic; not advanced
Primitive humans lived in caves and did not build their own homes.

7 **separate** *(adj)* different
There are three ***separate*** piles of items you can look at.

8 **spear** *(n)* a pointed weapon that is very long and can be thrown
Each soldier carried a sword and a ***spear***.

9 **tool** *(n)* a device used to do work
The lever is a basic ***tool*** that humans have used for a long time.

10 **trade** *(n)* the act of buying and selling goods
Kevin engages in ***trade*** in several different countries.

Unit 10

1 **battle** *(n)* a fight
The *Battle* of Marathon was very important in Greek history.

2 **block** *(v)* to stop someone or something from passing
We are going to *block* the government from tearing down the building.

3 **city-state** *(n)* an independent city that controls the land around it
Athens and Sparta were two powerful Greek *city-states*.

4 **compose** *(v)* to write; to create; to make
Mozart *composed* many great pieces of music.

5 **conquer** *(v)* to defeat; to win against
The Spanish *conquered* the Aztecs and Incas in the Americas.

6 **drop** *(v)* to let something fall to the ground
Do not *drop* that vase, or it will break.

7 **flee** *(v)* to run away
The villagers will probably *flee* when the army approaches.

8 **narrow** *(adj)* not wide; thin
The trail becomes very *narrow* near the top of the mountain.

9 **site** *(n)* a location; a place
Please tell me the *site* of the meeting.

10 **weaken** *(v)* to lose strength; to become weak
Mark is starting to *weaken* because of his illness.

Unit 11

1 **contagious** *(adj)* spreading easily to other people; able to be caught, like an illness
The flu is *contagious*, so stay away from those sick people.

2 **decade** *(n)* a period of ten years
Jenny has lived in Europe for the last *decade*.

3 **faith** *(n)* belief
You must have *faith* that this is going to work.

4 **laborer** *(n)* a worker
The company pays the *laborers* after they finish work each day.

5 **noble** *(n)* an aristocrat; a member of the upper class
Tim is a *noble*, but his family has little money.

6 **plague** *(n)* a disease that affects a large number of people at the same time
Thousands of people in Europe died because of the *plague*.

7 **previously** *(adv)* before; prior to
Previously, no one had ever heard of Sam.

8 **serf** *(n)* a peasant; a very poor person
Many *serfs* in the village did not get enough food to eat.

9 **suffer** *(v)* to experience a lot of pain
Chris *suffered* a lot of pain because of the car accident.

10 **survivor** *(n)* a person who lives through a dangerous event or time
There were a few *survivors* from the plane crash.

Unit 12

1 **announce** *(v)* to state out loud

We will ***announce*** the winner in just a moment.

2 **dramatically** *(adv)* seriously; severely

Anna changed her style ***dramatically*** last year.

3 **mythology** *(n)* a collection of stories from the past that may or may not be true

The students enjoy reading stories from Roman ***mythology***.

4 **primary** *(adj)* main; important

Tell us the ***primary*** goal of the project.

5 **reintroduce** *(v)* to provide something a second time

Officials will ***reintroduce*** wolves to some parts of the national park.

6 **scene** *(n)* a picture

The ***scene*** in this painting shows two ships on the sea.

7 **scholar** *(n)* an academic; a person who studies a great deal

Fred is a ***scholar*** who studies ancient Greek history.

8 **technique** *(n)* a method

What kind of ***technique*** did she use to make this painting?

9 **text** *(n)* a book or any other type of written material

Read the ***text*** to find out the information you need.

10 **topic** *(n)* a subject

You should choose a ***topic*** for your paper by this week.

Chapter 4 Landmarks

Unit 13

1 **construction** *(n)* the building of something

The ***construction*** of the bridge will take several months.

2 **debate** *(n)* an argument between two or more people

Joe and Steve will have a ***debate*** on the death penalty.

3 **enormous** *(adj)* very large; huge

Peter made an ***enormous*** amount of money thanks to his invention.

4 **major** *(adj)* important

The engine of the car has a ***major*** problem.

5 **monument** *(n)* a building or statue made in honor of a person or event

You can see many ***monuments*** in London, England.

6 **obelisk** *(n)* a narrow four-sided tower than ends with a pyramid on top

That ***obelisk*** is located in Egypt.

7 **organizer** *(n)* a person who helps get an event ready

Tell me the names of the ***organizers*** of the party.

8 **skyline** *(n)* the outline of buildings against the sky

I love looking at the ***skyline*** of the city.

9 **surrounding** *(adj)* nearby; close

Are there many businesses in the ***surrounding*** area?

10 **victory** *(n)* a win

Our team needs one more ***victory*** to make the playoffs.

Unit 14

1 **amazing** *(adj)* incredible; wonderful
It is ***amazing*** how kind Denise is.

2 **attend** *(v)* to go to
We are going to ***attend*** the soccer game tonight.

3 **cathedral** *(n)* a large Catholic church
The ***cathedral*** is the most impressive building in the city.

4 **fail** *(v)* to be unsuccessful
I ***failed*** to win the contest.

5 **floor** *(n)* a level of a building; a story
His office is located on the third ***floor***.

6 **renowned** *(adj)* famous; well-known
He is ***renowned*** for being a generous man.

7 **stable** *(adj)* steady; constant; not in danger of falling or breaking
The building is ***stable*** and will not collapse.

8 **stadium** *(n)* an arena; a large building in which people watch others play sports
How many people can fit in that ***stadium***?

9 **stage** *(n)* a period; a phase
The building is in the first ***stage*** of construction.

10 **tower** *(n)* a high building
The soldiers are keeping watch over the area from the ***tower***.

Unit 15

1 **alongside** *(prep)* by; beside; next to
The car is parked ***alongside*** the building.

2 **delay** *(n)* a wait; a setback
What was the reason for the ***delay***?

3 **design** *(n)* the plan of a building
The architect is working on the ***design*** of the airport.

4 **gem** *(n)* a valuable stone such as a diamond or ruby
Some people are digging for ***gems*** in this area.

5 **harbor** *(n)* an area of water by shore that is deep enough for ships to sail into
Several ships are sailing in the ***harbor***.

6 **import** *(v)* to bring in from another country
The company ***imports*** goods from abroad and sells them here.

7 **original** *(adj)* first
We decided to use the ***original*** plan.

8 **palace** *(n)* a large castle
Kings and queens lived in this ***palace*** for many years.

9 **precious** *(adj)* valuable; worth a lot
Gold and silver are two types of ***precious*** metals.

10 **tomb** *(n)* a burial chamber; a building in which a person is buried
There are many ***tombs*** of Egyptian pharaohs in the Valley of Kings.

Unit 16

1 **chain** *(n)* a series of metal rings connected to one another
The dog's owner puts a ***chain*** on his pet when he leaves the house.

2 **crown** *(n)* a type of headgear worn by a king or queen
The king's ***crown*** is made of gold.

3 **funding** *(n)* financial support; money used to pay for something
We need some more ***funding*** before we can start the project.

4 **goddess** *(n)* a female god
Athena, Hera, and Aphrodite were three Greek ***goddesses***.

5 **greet** *(v)* to say hello to
The teacher always ***greets*** her students in the morning.

6 **immigrate** *(v)* to move to a new country to live there
Many people ***immigrated*** to the United States in the 1800s.

7 **nervous** *(adj)* worried; anxious
Sarah always gets ***nervous*** before she takes a test.

8 **pedestal** *(n)* a base for a statue
The ***pedestal*** is made of marble.

9 **sculptor** *(n)* a person who makes statues or sculptures
That man is one of the world's best ***sculptors***.

10 **sight** *(n)* a view
The ***sight*** of the waterfall is a view he will not forget.

4 **biologist** *(n)* a person who studies biology
Jane is a ***biologist*** who studies animals living in forests.

5 **crater** *(n)* a large hole in the ground
There is a huge ***crater*** caused by a meteor impact.

6 **estimate** *(v)* to guess; to make a prediction
I ***estimate*** that it will take two hours to complete the assignment.

7 **extinct** *(adj)* no longer living
The dinosaurs are ***extinct***, so they no longer live on the Earth.

8 **predator** *(n)* an animal that hunts other animals, often for food
Sharks are some of the most dangerous ***predators*** in the water.

9 **preserve** *(n)* an area of land or water where the animals that live in it are protected
This area is a huge nature ***preserve***, so no hunting is allowed.

10 **vast** *(adj)* huge; enormous; very large
There are ***vast*** forests located in Siberia in Russia.

Chapter 5 The Ocean

Unit 17

1 **aquatic** *(adj)* relating to the water
Fish are ***aquatic*** animals that live their lives in the water.

2 **ban** *(v)* to forbid a person from doing something; to say that a person may not do something
The politician keeps trying to ***ban*** activities against the will of the people.

3 **bay** *(n)* a body of water next to shore that is protected by the land
The ship sailed into the ***bay*** and stayed there during the hurricane.

Unit 18

1 **conduct** *(v)* to do; to perform
The reporter is ***conducting*** an interview with the movie star.

2 **dive** *(n)* a trip below the surface of the water
They will make a ***dive*** by using their scuba gear.

3 **explore** *(v)* to travel around and look at an area; to sightsee
We plan to ***explore*** the region tomorrow.

4 **island** *(n)* land that has water all around it
My family is taking a trip to an ***island*** this summer.

5 **similar** *(adj)* alike; almost the same

Dave and Chris are very ***similar***, so many people think they are twins.

6 **solo** *(adj)* alone; by oneself

She likes to make ***solo*** trips during her vacations.

7 **submersible** *(n)* a machine such as a submarine that can travel under the water

This ***submersible*** can dive thousands of meters beneath the ocean's surface.

8 **survey** *(v)* to map or chart a region; to study an area in depth

We must ***survey*** the area before we make any buildings.

9 **vent** *(n)* an opening in the ground from which air or water comes out

There are some hot-water ***vents*** near that underwater volcano.

10 **width** *(n)* wideness; the size of something from one side to the other

The ***width*** of this building should be at least twenty meters.

Unit 19

1 **atmosphere** *(n)* the air

There is a lot of nitrogen in the Earth's ***atmosphere***.

2 **desert** *(n)* a region that gets very little rain or snow each year

The Sahara ***Desert*** in Africa is extremely hot.

3 **evolve** *(v)* slowly to change over time

Some animals ***evolve*** to adapt to their environments.

4 **fossil** *(n)* the remains, often bones, of an animal or plant

We like to dig for ***fossils*** near the river.

5 **harmful** *(adj)* damaging; dangerous; causing injury

Eating too much junk food can be ***harmful*** to your health.

6 **microbe** *(n)* an organism so small that one needs a microscope to see it

Many kinds of ***microbes*** are dangerous to humans.

7 **resemble** *(v)* to look or act like something else

Jim ***resembles*** his father when he smiles.

8 **shallow** *(adj)* low, not deep

The water in this part of the pool is very ***shallow***.

9 **shore** *(n)* the land next to a body of water such as an ocean, river, or lake

There are many animals next to the ***shore*** of the lake.

10 **sunlight** *(n)* the light that comes from the sun

It is bright during the day thanks to the ***sunlight***.

Unit 20

1 **apparently** *(adv)* seemingly; as far as one knows

Apparently, there is no one using this room.

2 **calm** *(adj)* peaceful; quiet; not loud or active

Today, the sea is very ***calm*** with no waves.

3 **gills** *(n)* the organs on fish that allow them to breathe underwater

The ***gills*** of fish are on both sides of their bodies.

4 **impossible** *(adj)* not able to happen

Right now, it is ***impossible*** to travel to the stars.

5 **man-eater** *(n)* an animal that attacks, kills, and eats humans

Lions and tigers are both ***man-eaters***.

6 **prey** *(n)* an animal that is hunted by other animals

Many small animals in the forest are ***prey*** for larger animals.

7 **properly** *(adv)* correctly; right

You need to solve the problem ***properly*** to get the correct answer.

8 **suddenly** *(adv)* quickly; instantly; without any warning

Suddenly, the cat attacked the mouse.

9 **wave** *(v)* to move one's arms back and forth, often in greeting

We ***waved*** to our friend when we saw him at the train station.

10 **witness** *(n)* a person who sees an event take place

Lucy is a ***witness*** who saw everything that happened.

memo

memo